Budget DTP on the Acorn Archimedes

by Roger Amos

Budget DTP on the Acorn Archimedes

Published by
David Bradforth
16 Rodney Way
Romford
Essex
RM7 8PD

Email: dave.bradforth@gmail.com

Printed by CreateSpace, an Amazon.com company.

Pubished by Alligata Media, Romford.

ISBN-13: 978-1511684842
ISBN-10: 1511684844

Contents

1: Introduction   4

2: What is DTP   6

3: Hardware and Software Needed and Recommended   11

4: A Quick Taste   13

5: !Draw in depth   15

6: Creating the text   27

7: The Font System   33

8: Page Layout   40

9: Sprites, !Paint and Clip Art   54

10: Understanding Printers   60

11: Reproducing your Work   67

12: Troubleshooting   73

13: The Next Step   79

Appendix: Glossary of DTP, Printing and Typographical Terms   81

1: Introduction

The Acorn Archimedes and A3000 computers are "naturals" for Desk Top Publishing (DTP) as they have the necessary large memories, excellent graphics facilities, high-speed processor and WIMP (Windows/Icons/Menus/Pointer) based operating system.

Suitable DTP packages are now available but none of these packages is cheap. Their prices, all in the £100 to £200 range, are hardly a barrier to the serious business or educational user, but do deter the home user or very small business wishing to experiment.

There is, however, a way to perform DTP-type operations on the Archimedes or A3000 at little or no extra cost and perfectly legally. The "applications suite" which comes with the RISC OS operating system includes !Draw, an object-based drawing package, and !Edit a text editor.

!Draw possesses the graphics and page layout features of DTP, but it has no facilities for text editing. !Edit, in contrast, allows the editing of text files but has very limited provision for formatting them. The two applications can work together, however; !Edit being used to create and edit text and !Draw to lay it out and add graphics. The Archimedes User Guide mentions, almost casually, that !Draw's "text area objects" make possible "simple desktop publishing". Many RISC OS users have enthusiastically tried out this "simple DTP" capability which offers the prospect of producing professional-looking documentation using software which they already own and saving them the need to purchase an expensive "proper" DTP package. Some have succeeded but many have found themselves frustrated.

The frustration arises from a number of causes; the following are typical.

- The User Manual gives little information and in places is confusing.
- A whole new "language" of textual commands must be mastered.
- Editing "text area objects" in !Draw is impossible.
- The range of fonts provided with RISC OS is very limited.
- The system persistently gives error messages such as "Bad font number" whose cause can be very difficult to find.
- When the page is at last composed, the printer produces gobbledegook.
- Even when the printer reproduces a recognisable page, print quality is poor.

Yes, there are many pitfalls and there is much to learn. When all is said and done, !Draw is not a DTP system. It will never give you the convenience of a "proper" DTP package. If you want that convenience, you must pay the price!

But there are simple "fixes" to all the problems listed above, except the second. If you have patience, !Draw will give remarkable results. In fact any page layout that can be produced using a full DTP package can also be produced in !Draw, although it will probably take longer and some effects may require the use of additional software. And indeed !Draw can do some things that DTP packages cannot do.

I started using !Draw and !Edit to produce user manuals, company newsletters and other publications while waiting for the software industry to introduce a DTP package that would run reliably on my one-megabyte machine. I confess that I came close to throwing the computer system out of the window on several occasions – once I wasted a whole day trying to find the cause of the 'Bad font number* error. In time I have learned the solutions to most of the problems commonly encountered and also many shortcuts. This book draws on my experience.

I am also indebted to many friends and organisations with whom I have swapped notes and shared experiences.

2: What is DTP?

Desktop Publishing (DTP) is the latest in a chain of developments that arguably began with the invention of paper and the quill pen. Ever since then people have used a succession of increasingly sophisticated tools to put text and graphics on paper.

A Short History of Mechanised Writing

The Typewriter

The mechanical typewriter, which originated in the USA during the latter half of the 19th century, represented the first major advance over pen or pencil. It offered two principal advantages over these.

Firstly, a competent typist could write much faster with a typewriter than with pen or pencil, so boosting office productivity.

Secondly, writing produced on a typewriter was consistent and clearly legible. Some might regret the lack of the "individuality" in handwriting, but nevertheless, as a vehicle for business or technical communications its benefits were unquestionable. The reader of scrawling handwritten script which included unfamiliar words such as technical terms or foreign names was, and still is, frequently compelled to guess what was intended. The typewriter eliminated this–and often obviated the acute embarrassment occasioned when visiting foreign VIPs found their names unrecognisably mis-spelt!

It was not surprising, then, that the typewriter heralded an "office revolution" as far-reaching in its effects as the industrial revolution that had preceded it (and which made it possible). Typewriter manufacturers made fortunes in this, the first "business machine" boom. Some of their names, such as Olivetti, are still associated with business machines today. Typing became part of the school curriculum and, especially amongst women, a favoured occupation. You can still buy a brand new mechanical typewriter. Its design, however, would probably raise few eyebrows if inspected by resurrected typewriter designers from a century ago. Inevitably there have been some advances over the years, such as the option of electrical power to remove some of the physical effort needed. The

Vari-Typer and later daisywheel and golfball machines offered interchangeable typefaces. Recently on some sophisticated machines electronics have been introduced between keyboard and paper to allow advanced correction facilities. However, these features were really borrowed from the next generation of writing machine, the wordprocessor.

Despite its many advantages, the mechanical typewriter suffered one major drawback. You could summarise the flowchart of data in a typewriter by the diagram shown below. As soon as the typist hit the key, the character was on the paper. And when it was on the paper, it was not easy to change it.

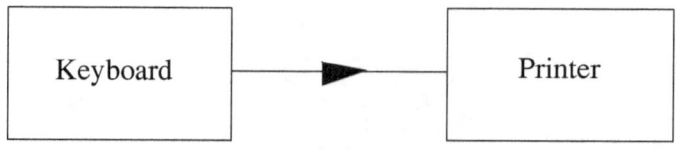

Block diagram of a typewriter

Now even the best typists make mistakes from time to time. Many essential typewriter users would readily admit that they are not good typists. One journalist with only two-finger typing ability reckoned that to type a news item took him 10 minutes, to correct it took 10 more minutes and to correct the corrections took a further 10 minutes. More time was taken up with correction than with the original text!

Some corrections, such as substituting one character for another or deleting an unwanted character, were possible using rubbers, correction fluid or chalk-covered correction paper. But corrections made by these means were clearly visible on the final copy, making it appear untidy. Many offices had "house rules" about the number of such corrections permitted in a document that was going outside the organisation. For example, if there were more than two corrections on the page, the unfortunate typist was compelled to retype the whole page, repeating largely the same keystrokes.

Other types of correction, such as the insertion of a word or, worse still, the insertion of a whole new paragraph, were clearly impossible. These demanded that the whole document be retyped. What was needed was an automatic typewriter with a memory–a memory whose contents could easily be edited–so that it could do all the retyping by itself.

The Wordprocessor

Computers provided the technology needed to do this. Typesetters were the first to avail themselves of it for editing text being prepared for typesetting. But it was not until the early 1980s that the dream began to become a reality for ordinary office workers, schools and domestic users. This was a consequence of the advances in technology which made microcomputers affordable.

Most wordprocessors are general-purpose microcomputers running wordprocessing software. There are some dedicated wordprocessing machines, but they are essentially microcomputers in which the wordprocessing software is "built in" and which may lack any means of running other kinds of software.

A wordprocessor is a system which has a keyboard more or less like a typewriter's on which text can be typed. As text is typed, it appears on a monitor screen and is also entered into the computer's memory. As more text is typed, the first lines typed may disappear off the top of the screen, but they are still in memory and can be brought back on to the screen if required.

The main advance was that the contents of computer memory, unlike the contents of a sheet of paper, can easily be changed. On a wordprocessor, a mistake in an earlier line can readily be corrected, even if it involves the insertion of additional text. Whole paragraphs can be inserted, moved, copied, or deleted. "Search and replace" facilities allow the entire document to be searched for occurrences of, perhaps, a repeated mis-spelling, the correct version being automatically substituted.

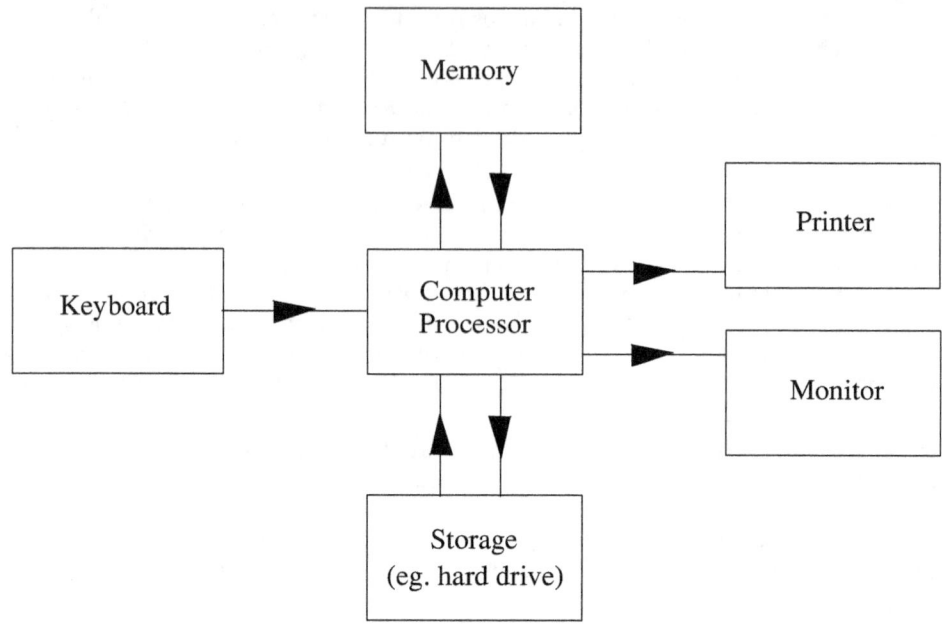

Block diagram of a wordprocessor

When the operator is satisfied that the document, as shown on the screen, is correct, then it is printed out. Murphy's Law demands that, as the paper comes off the printer, some appalling mistake is spotted that was missed on the screen! But it's easy enough to correct this on screen, discard the original sheets and print out a copy of the corrected version. Moreover, the document can be stored for future reference or re-use on such storage media as floppy disc or hard disc. The picture above shows the possible interactions.

The word processor opened up many exciting new business possibilities. For example, it made possible the printing of many copies of the same document, each with minor alterations. A company could send its customers personalised reminder letters about unpaid invoices. The same basic text would be used in each letter, with just the recipient's name, address, account number and outstanding sum being changed. Many wordprocessor packages allowed 'mailmerge' in which the changeable items are listed separately and then automatically inserted in the right places before printing out the document. If the printer had automatic paper feed, the system could be left unattended, churning out important business letters whose production only a few years previously would have required many painstaking hours of typists' work.

A sad by-product of this technology is the personalised junk mail that many folk receive every week, informing them of the huge cash prize or luxury car that they may have already won if they opt to buy the described encyclopaedia, record collection or whatever. Indeed, far from ushering in the long-heralded age of the "paperless office", computers have done more for the paper industry than any previous invention except the printing press.

On early wordprocessors, the screen display bore only a passing resemblance to the final printed document. As software and hardware became more sophisticated, "WYSIWYG" became the accepted standard. This acronym stands for "What You See Is What You Get". It means that the screen display gives an accurate idea of the appearance of the finished document. The displayed typeface may not be identical to that used by the printer, but such effects as bold, underline and italic should be represented on screen. In addition, the effects of the margins, indents and tab stops which control the position of text should be correctly displayed.

Wordprocessing is still one of the most widely used applications of microcomputers. It has the advantage of comparative simplicity. But it has limitations. Most wordprocessors cannot handle graphics. They can only print out documents using the printer's built-in character sets. At best the printout will look as if it has come off a sophisticated typewriter. And, indeed, the wordprocessor is ultimately a very sophisticated typewriter.

Desktop Publishing

The next step took the dream a stage further. Why not use the microcomputer to create documents in which the text uses proportionally spaced characters in a range of typefaces, styles and sizes, as well as graphics such as lines, boxes, circles, line drawings and even half-tone illustrations? Indeed why not handle all the same kinds of material reproduced by professional publishers and printers in the magazines, newspapers and brochures that we read every day? This would allow organisations to produce professional-looking newsletters, brochures and posters in-house—work which until then had always been the specialist province of the graphic design and printing industries. This is what became known as *Desktop Publishing* (DTP).

DTP is a far more demanding application than word processing. A DTP package normally offers most of the facilities of a wordprocessor, but also many more. For example, in DTP most often the printer uses its graphics capability to reproduce text using the images of typefaces stored in the computer rather than reproducing its built-in typefaces. To achieve an appearance which even begins to resemble professional typesetting the graphics must be at a resolution of at least 300 dots per inch. Now in wordprocessing, for the computer to tell the printer to print a letter "W" it normally needs to send the printer only eight bits which is sufficient to identify the character. In DTP to print a 12 point "W" at 300 dots per inch the computer may need to send as many as 2500 bits. This is because it is sending the printer the data required to build up an image of the character dot by dot. The development of DTP has inevitably marched hand-in-glove with the development of high- resolution graphics output devices such as laser printers. So for DTP, computers must be capable of processing massive quantities of data very rapidly.

The first DTP package was Aldus Pagemaker for the Apple Macintosh, released in July 1985. The Aldus company had been formed early in 1984 by Paul Brainerd and four of his colleagues who had worked with him at a company called Atex. This company specialised in text processing systems for minicomputers. The creation of Pagemaker involved the interaction of Paul Brainerd's team with two other groups of people; a team from Adobe who had devised the PostScript page description language for laser printers and the Apple team led by Steve Jobs which created the Macintosh.

The Macintosh, rather than the IBM PC which had already been around for two or three years, was chosen as the original computer for Pagemaker because it offered the first interactive graphics interface. In wordprocessing no graphics interface was needed, as the application was in general concerned only with text and not with graphics. But in DTP the page is built up on screen WYSIWYG style and the user must have the facility to place text or graphics at any position on the page with very high accuracy. Clearly this needed much finer control than could conveniently be provided through the cursor keys. This fine control was possible through the Macintosh's "WIMP" environment.

WIMP stands for "Windows, Icons, Menus and Pointer", a system familiar to anyone who has used the Desktop environment provided by RISC OS computers. Windows are areas of the screen set apart for certain applications. Icons are small pictures on the screen which represent applications, utilities or facilities. Menus are lists of available options. A mouse provides fine control of the position on screen of the pointer. To select a facility, you move the mouse until the pointer is over the appropriate icon or option and then click a button on the mouse.

For graphics work the WIMP environment offered obvious advantages and similar systems were soon available for many other machines. For example, "Microsoft Windows" was developed for the IBM PC. A version of Pagemaker for the PC followed some months later. This was followed by a succession of DTP packages, many of which are now household names, mainly for the IBM PC and compatibles.

Acorn's earlier computers such as the BBC Model B and the Master Series did not have the power to handle full DTP, although several software packages for these did provide some DTP-like functions. It was not until the advent of the Archimedes and its derivatives that Acorn users could indulge in true DTP. These machines with their comparatively large memories, fast processor and WIMP environment might have been especially created with DTP in mind.

3 : Hardware and Software Needed and Recommended

You will need a RISC OS computer having at least one megabyte of RAM. You will also need a printer. Most popular dot-matrix types can be used, but whether their quality is acceptable depends on what you are attempting to do. You will need a laser printer or an inkjet printer if you wish to fully exploit the system's capability. If you have a suitable computer, you will probably already have the following software, supplied with the machine or with RISC OS if obtained subsequently:

- !Edit
- !Draw
- Fonts
- !Printers
- !Paint

The above represents the absolute minimum requirement for the DTP activities described in this book.

Outline Fonts

The most important items to obtain is a selection of outline fonts.

Outline fonts are stored as plotting instructions which are independent of font size. The result is smooth, perfectly shaped characters at any size, both on screen and on paper. The illustration below contrasts a large point sized "A" in Trinity Medium produced by the old bitmap system with the same character produced from the outline font system. The improvement could hardly be more obvious. Even 12-point print from the outline font system is noticeably better than that from the bitmap system.

This was printed using
a bitmap font system

This was printed using the
RISC OS outline font system

With the introduction of RISC OS 3 with the A5000 the outline font system was adopted as the standard for the Acorn computer family and many outline fonts are available. As well as commercial fonts there are a large number of public domain outline fonts in circulation, but their quality is not as good as that of the commercial products.

All these outline fonts may be used with !Draw and !Edit, and if you should subsequently decide to purchase a full DTP package, you will be able to use all your outline fonts with that too.

Manipulating Outline Fonts

When you have the Outline Font Manager, there are two further items of software that you should consider purchasing. The first is !FontFX previously from The Data Store, now from APDL, price about £10. This allows you to perform an almost infinite range of manipulations and special effects using outline fonts. Its use is considered in more detail in Chapter 8.

The other is the Font Editor application, !FontEd. This Acorn application is available free. Its original purpose was the creation of new outline fonts and the modification of existing ones. However, it can also be used to convert outline font characters to !Draw-compatible path objects, making possible a more limited range of the same kinds of effect as produced by !FontFX.

(Note that !FontEd is now rather old and is not really suitable for use with later high quality Acorn fonts. !DrFonty or !FontFiend from APDL.org.uk are much better alternatives).

4 : A Quick Taste

As already mentioned, DTP using !Draw and !Edit is not quite as simple and convenient as that using a full DTP package. In a full DTP package, almost as soon as you have loaded the application you can begin typing on a blank page, making corrections or amendments to previous lines, just as in a wordprocessor. DTP using !Draw and !Edit, however, is essentially a two-stage process, the first using !Edit to prepare your text and the second using !Draw to lay it out. Some corrections may force you back from the later stage to the earlier stage. You can, however, have both !Edit and !Draw installed simultaneously so that the transfer of data between them is quick and easy.

This chapter gives you a brief over-view of the steps involved in creating and printing a single-page document consisting of body text, a few headings and graphics. Inevitably many details and many of the facilities available to you have been omitted–these will be described in later chapters.

This chapter assumes that you are reasonably familiar with the RISC OS Desktop environment.

Load both !Edit and !Draw. Even on a one megabyte machine with the font cache expanded it is possible to have both installed simultaneously, but you may need to restrict yourself to a screen mode that is not too demanding on memory. If you have a multi-sync monitor, use Mode 19 (80K) or even Mode 18 (40K) instead of Mode 20 (160K). This is quite adequate in the early stages of writing and editing text.

Open an !Edit window (by clicking SELECT on the !Edit icon) and compose your main text. Don't worry about main headings at this stage, just enter the "body text" with its sub-headings, if any. Your text must begin with the special "header" (described in Chapter 6) that defines font choices, line spacing and justification type. If you regularly use the same selection of fonts, font styles and font sizes I suggest that you keep a standard "header" file on disc which you can load as a starter for each document.

Once your text is written, check it through for mistakes and correct any that you see. Save your text to disc.

Leaving your !Edit window open, now open a !Draw window (by clicking SELECT on the !Draw icon). With the pointer in the !Draw window click on MENU and display the "Misc" sub-menu and then the "Paper limits" sub-menu. Select your required paper size, orientation (portrait or landscape) and then select "Show". (If you use ADJUST to select your choices, the menu will remain open instead of disappearing after each selection.)

Now save your text file into !Draw. You do this by selecting "Save" in !Edit in the normal manner but instead of dragging the icon into a directory viewer, drag it into the Draw window. If you get an error message, see Chapter 12 on "Troubleshooting".

Lay out your text roughly. How to do this is described in Chapter 8. Don't worry at this stage about getting its positioning exactly right; there will be time for that later. Check that text is correctly spelt and punctuated and that the style (font name, font size etc) are correct. If you spot mistakes, return to your !Edit window, correct the text or header there and transfer it to !Draw again, making sure that you drag the icon over the existing text area so that the corrected text replaces the original.

When you are sure that the text is correct and laid out in roughly the right places, you can now concentrate on getting your layout exactly right, eg ensuring that adjacent columns start at the same height etc. Insert any graphics and any headings using text objects. These are described in Chapters 5 and 8. When the page is laid out to your satisfaction, you are ready to print it. First save your page to disc if you have not already done so. Now print your page using the "Print" option in the "Misc" sub-menu.

(Murphy's law demands that you will at once spot a major error which you never noticed on the screen!)

5 : !Draw In Depth

!Draw is an *object* based drawing package. Everything that appears in a !Draw window is an *object* or part of an object.

There are two quite different ways in which art programs can store the artwork which they produce and the RISC OS applications suite contains an example of each. One way is to divide the picture into a two-dimensional array of uniformly sized dots or cells each being assigned a single colour. These cells are called "picture elements" but are more commonly known by the abbreviation "pixels". A bank of memory contains details of the array size and stores numbers representing the colour of each pixel. The pixels often correspond to the dots that make up the screen display itself, but need not always do so.

!Paint is an example of this type of program. It has the advantage of comparative simplicity, but there are several distinct disadvantages. Firstly, if the pixel resolution corresponds to a high-resolution screen display, the artwork will take up vast quantities of memory. A full- screen size picture in Mode 20, for example, would take 160 Kilobytes. Secondly, the pixel structure itself is the limit of resolution; you will not see more detail by magnifying the screen display. Increasing the magnification factor on the "zoom" facility will simply make the pixel- based structure more obvious. Thirdly, the display is purely "two dimensional". What you see on the screen is all there is. If you overlay part of your design with new material, the concealed matter is lost irretrievably.

The other way to store artwork is to save not the finished screen display, but rather the instructions that were used to create it. Whenever the drawing or a part of it is redrawn or printed, the instructions used to create it are executed afresh.

!Draw is an example of this type of program. This method has the advantage that it is entirely independent of screen mode, comparatively miserly in its use of memory, it allows infinitely fine detail and one part of the drawing may overlie another without destroying it. Since the specifications for the obscured detail are still present in the file, moving or deleting the overlying object will reveal once again the matter that was previously obscured. There is one disadvantage. Scrolling and printing become appreciably slower as more objects are added to the drawing, because these necessarily involve the fresh execution of all the instructions used to make up the picture. Nevertheless all serious DTP software works on this object- based principle.

Objects

A !Draw file, then, consists of a sequence of "blocks" of data each containing all of the information needed to reconstruct one of the objects that make up the drawing. Their sequence in the file normally follows the chronological order in which the objects were added to the drawing. Each time !Draw redraws a screen or prints a page it retraces the steps by which the drawing was created, except of course that it omits any objects that have been deleted from the file. There is no limit to the number of objects in a drawing apart from the availability of computer memory. Four types of object can be included in a !Draw file:

- Path objects, i.e., line drawings created in !Draw or imported from compatible applications such as !FontFX.

- Text objects, i.e., single lines of text created in !Draw.
- Text area objects, i.e., multi-line blocks of text created in !Edit.
- Sprites, i.e., pixel-based graphics such as those created or edited in !Paint.

!Draw's art features are well described in the Acorn User Manual and so only a brief description will be given here.

The Main Menu

!Draw's main menu is accessed by clicking MENU while the pointer is in the !Draw window. All of the application's facilities can be accessed through this menu, but there are also "shortcut" routes to some of them through the toolbox which users may find more convenient. All but one of the menu items lead to further sub-menus, which will be described later.

Misc

This leads to a sub-menu concerned mainly with page size, orientation and printing. The "New view" option is also accessed from this sub-menu, which is considered later.

Save

This leads to a sub-menu concerned with the export of data. This includes saving complete drawings to the current filing system and exporting data to other applications or other !Draw windows. The first option saves the whole of the current sheet. The second option saves "selected" objects as !Draw files–see later under "Select Mode". The third and fourth options save sprites and text areas respectively as sprite files and text files. Only one sprite or text area at a time can be saved and each must first be "selected".

In each case enter a file name (or use the one offered) and then drag the icon into the appropriate directory viewer or application window. If the item has been saved before, to save it again simply click SELECT on "OK".

The facility to export data into other applications is particularly useful. Subject to the availability of memory this allows you to transfer a selected drawing into another !Draw window, or a sprite into ! Paint for editing or a text area back into !Edit for editing without any need to save it to disc.

Style

This leads to a double sub-menu concerned with the "style" of the object being entered. The top half relates to the style of path objects (see later) and the bottom half to text objects (see later).

Enter

This allows you to change the type of data you are entering. In practice it is an alternative to clicking on the items in the toolbox, that is the column of nine icons down the left-hand edge of the screen, which provides a generally quicker and more convenient route. See later under "Toolbox".

Select

Clicking on "Select" has the same effect as clicking on the bottom item in the toolbox to enter "Select mode" and then clicking "menu". For further information and for details on the sub-menu which appears see below under "Select Mode".

Zoom

This takes you to a dialogue box which allows you to select the ratio of size of screen display to that of the drawing, i.e. the magnification in the current window. You can magnify the screen image in order to get a more detailed display of part of the window or you can reduce it so that you see more of the sheet, perhaps even the whole sheet, on which you are working.

The left-hand number represents the screen display size and the right-hand number the actual sheet size. Thus 4:1 represents a screen display magnified to four times normal size and 1:5 represents a reduced-scale screen display one fifth of normal size. The maximum magnification or reduction factor is 8.

Magnifying greatly reduces the speed of scrolling, especially in text areas, where its use is not recommended. For graphics, however, it can be very useful as it allows lines or boxes to be aligned or abutted very accurately.

A reduced-scale view of the whole sheet can also be useful. The "New View" facility accessed via the "Misc" menu opens a second window on to the same sheet which, suitably reduced, can be used for this purpose. Any operation in either window will affect the sheet and will be displayed in both.

Grid

The grid is a pattern of dots superimposed over the screen image as an aid to the measurement and accurate alignment of objects. A particularly useful feature of !Draw, the grid does not appear in printouts. To display the grid select "Show" on the "Grid" sub-menu. Selecting "Lock" causes all new objects to lock themselves on to the nearest grid point. The grid colour can be changed from the menu as can the spacing of the points.

There are two grades of grid point: major divisions which are shown as little "+" signs and subdivisions which are shown as dots. There is a choice of inch and metric scales for the major divisions and you can choose as many subdivisions as you wish per major division. The default is one inch for major divisions and four subdivisions per inch. These measurements relate to the size of the final printout and not the screen display which is of course affected by both monitor type and zoom setting. For geometrical purposes an "isometric" (triangular) pattern of grid is also available.

You are strongly recommended to engage "Grid lock" before drawing horizontal and vertical rules on the page. This will ensure that the lines are absolutely horizontal or vertical. If you simply trust that lines which appear horizontal or vertical on the screen are indeed so, you may have a nasty surprise when you print out your page. The printer, remember, probably has a much higher resolution than the screen and will reproduce discrepancies too small to show on the screen. If you omit "Grid Lock", you can always select the item and use the "Snap to grid" facility later.

Toolbox This toggles the toolbox on and off. You will probably find it useful to leave the toolbox on for most of the time, but this facility allows you to turn it off when you wish to examine or draw on the part of the sheet which it obscures.

Misc Menu

The "Misc" sub-menu consists of four items.

Info

This simply displays information about the version of !Draw in use.

New view

This opens a new window onto the page being created. Any operations performed in either window are effective on the same sheet and so will be reflected in both windows. The second window can be used to display a different part of the same sheet or it can be used to show a reduced-scale (using "Zoom") image of the entire page. The latter is most useful in showing at a glance the whereabouts, for instance, of selected objects.

Paper limits

This leads to a further sub-menu. "Show" highlights the area of the page that will be printed, provided that the appropriate printer driver is, or has been, installed. This is especially important if you have chosen to work on a large sheet size, such as A2, when your printer can handle only A4. The area that will be printed is highlighted by a grey tinted surround (shown in solid black in two-colour modes). Only items enclosed by the tinted area are printed–any item in the tinted area or outside it will be omitted by the printer. To print a larger sheet than the printer can handle you will need to "Select all" and drag the entire contents of the sheet to bring each part of it in turn into the indicated area for printing.

"Portrait" and "Landscape" refer to the two possible orientations of the paper. Portrait has the long axis upright (as in most portrait paintings) and Landscape has the long axis horizontal (as in most landscape paintings). !Draw allows you to create and print pages having either orientation. A tick appears beside the option currently selected–clicking SELECT on the unselected option selects it.

Next there follows a selection of sheet sizes ranging from A0 down to A5. Again a tick appears beside the currently selected size. The default setting is A4 landscape. By choosing a larger size than your intended page size you can treat a multi-page document as though it were all one very large page, but this will result in slow scrolling and printing.

Print

The dialogue box header displays the name of the current printer driver. If none is installed, the header reads "not present". A prompt for the number of copies to be printed is, sadly, ignored in version 0.44. To begin printing, click on the bottom "print" icon.

The Toolbox

On the left-hand edge of the !Draw window is a column of nine icons, illustrated below. This is called the toolbox. If you find it gets in the way, you can remove it by clicking MENU and clicking SELECT on the bottom item. Toolbox. Click on this again to get the toolbox back. The toolbox provides a valuable set of shortcuts to 'Draw's "enter" and SELECT facilities. It is useful to consider the bottom icon first.

	Straight line
	Straight line with autoclose
	Curved line
	Curved line with autoclose
	Move (no line)
	Elipse
	Rectangle
	Text
	Select mode

Select Mode

Clicking on the bottom icon, the one containing an arrow, enters SELECT mode, one of the most useful facilities in !Draw. It can also be entered from the main menu by clicking on select. Select mode allows one or more objects to be "selected". When selected, objects can be subjected to a diversity of interesting operations which will be considered shortly.

There are four ways an object can become selected. Note that these apply only when in "select mode".

- If you wish to select one object only, move the pointer over that object and click SELECT. Any objects that were previously selected will be de-selected.
- If you wish select an additional object when one or more objects are already selected, move the pointer over the object concerned and click ADJUST. This object will now be selected in addition to those that were previously selected.
- If you wish to select all the objects in the drawing, click MENU, display the "Select" sub-menu and click on "Select all".
- If you wish to select all the objects in a certain area of the drawing, move the pointer to a nearby position where it is not over any object, hold down SELECT and drag out a box (exactly like the rectangle creation mode described later). All objects overlapping the box when you release SELECT become selected. Any objects that were previously selected and which are wholly outside the box are de-selected.

Objects that have been selected are distinguished by the appearance around their edges of a dotted red boundary box having two "handles" on its right-hand edge. The significance of these handles will be explained shortly.

Objects can be de-selected in the following ways:

- If you wish to de-select just one object, move the pointer over that object and click ADJUST. If other objects were previously selected, they will remain selected.
- Click SELECT over another object. That object becomes selected and all others are de-selected.

- Click SELECT with the pointer not over any object. All objects that were selected are de-selected.
- On the "Select" sub-menu click on "Clear". This de-selects all objects.
- On the toolbox, click on a different icon so that you leave select mode. This de-selects all objects.

Note that the Select mechanism does not always work as efficiently as the User Manual leads one to expect, especially where the objects concerned are parts of a text area. Where many objects overlap, it can at times be very difficult to select the particular object you want. A useful trick is to use the "box" method to select all objects in the vicinity and then click ADJUST on all the unwanted objects to de-select them until only the one you wish to select remains selected.

So what can you do to selected items7

You can *move* them. Move the pointer within the red dotted boundary box and hold down SELECT. The colour or the dotted boundary changes and you can now use the mouse to drag the object, releasing SELECT when it is in its chosen new position. Note that if other objects are also selected, they too will be moved an equal distance in the same direction. If all objects are selected, the entire contents of the drawing will be moved and there are many operations in DTP where this facility is useful, such as in printing out a multi-page document.

You can *scale* the objects. Move the pointer into the lower of the two handles on the right-hand edge of the dotted red boundary. Hold down SELECT and drag the object's bottom right-hand corner to its chosen new position. The top left-hand corner will remain in its original location so that the object's height and width are changed. If the object is a path object or a sprite, it can he inverted or mirror-imaged by dragging its bottom over its top or its right-hand edge over its left-hand edge. Note, however, that text objects and text areas cannot be inverted or mirror-imaged. The effect ot scaling on text area objects is rather special and is considered later 11 other objects are selected they too will be scaled in equal proportion.

You can change the *style characteristics* if the object is a path object (line drawing) or text object. Changes selected from the top half of the "Style" sub-menu, such as new line widths, line colours or fill colours, will be applied to all selected path objects. Changes selected from the bottom half of the sub-menu, such as new font names, text colours or font sizes, will be applied to all selected text objects. Note that while you can edit the structure of a single selected path object by selecting the "Edit" option from the "Select" sub-menu, you cannot edit the contents of a text object.

You can *rotate* them if they are path objects (line drawings). Move the pointer into the upper of the two handles on the right-hand edge of the dotted red boundary. By dragging it you will find that the selected object rotates as though it were pivoted at its mid-point. If other objects are selected, they too will be rotated through an equal angle. Note, however, that text objects, text area objects and sprites cannot be rotated.

The following operations are accessed from the "Select" sub-menu of the main menu. Some options may not be applicable and will be shown in faint type. If no objects are selected, only the top item, "Select all", will be available.

- **Select all** - This causes all objects in the drawing to become selected.

20

- **Clear** - This causes all objects in the drawing to become deselected.
- **Copy** - This creates a copy of each selected item, slightly offset from the original. The copy is selected, but not the original. This is a very useful facility as its repeated use allows large numbers of identical objects to be built up!
- **Delete** - This permanently removes all selected objects. After "Select all" it will completely destroy all objects, leaving you with an empty sheet. It does not issue a warning first! So use it with care, checking first that only those objects which you wish to remove are selected.
- **Front** - This moves selected objects to the front of the diagram so that they obscure any other objects which they overlap.
- **Back** - This moves selected objects to the back of the diagram so that they are obscured by any other objects which they overlap.
- **Group** - This only applies if more than one object is selected. It causes all the selected objects to be treated as though they were one object with a common boundary box.
- **Ungroup** - This reverses the effect of the last described operation, separating a previously grouped object into its constituent objects. It only applies if a single grouped object is selected.
- **Edit** - This only applies if a single path object is selected. It allows the object to be edited, eg its points and control points become visible and can be adjusted.
- **Snap to grid** - This only applies if the grid is displayed and grid lock is active. It forces each point in the selected objects to snap on to the nearest grid points.
- **Justify** - This only applies to groups. It allows, for example, the constituents of a title page to be neatly centred or ranged left or ranged right. It is particularly useful for ensuring that multiple headings using text objects are accurately centred or neatly aligned on the left.
- **Rotate** - This allows you rotate the selected object(s) through a specified number of degrees anti-clockwise. Note, however, that text objects, text area objects and sprites cannot be rotated.
- **X scale** and **Y scale** - These allow you to scale the selected object(s) by a known exact figure rather than the inexact amount obtained by dragging the lower "handle". The figure is in proportion to the current size. Thus entering 2.0 will double that dimension and entering 0.5 will halve it. The X-scale relates to the horizontal axis and the Y-scale to the vertical.
- **Line scale** - This scales the width of the lines in the selected paths. Scaling is relative to current line width.
- **Magnify** - This combines into one operation X scale, Y scale and Line scale. Line scale is unaffected if the original line width is set to "Thin".

The Four Types of 'Object'

1. Path Objects

The top five icons in the toolbox are used to create "path objects" step by step. The sixth and seventh icons create ready-made path objects. A path object is a drawing made up of a series of "paths". A path may be a straight line, a curved line or a move that does not draw a line at all. You may build up a path object freely changing between the different types of path as you go.

The top icon gives simple straight lines. Place the pointer where you want your line to start and click SELECT; if you are dissatisfied with your starting point, click ADJUST and the line will be cancelled. With your line started, now move the pointer to the position where you wish your line to end and click SELECT again. This fixes the end of the line and also provisionally starts a second line. Click ADJUST if you wish to finish your object. Lines are shown in pale grey while still provisional; they change to the currently selected line colour when finished.

The second icon also gives straight lines but with one difference– "auto-close". This means that when you finish your object by clicking ADJUST an extra line is inserted automatically between the current pointer position and the beginning of the first line, closing the shape. You can draw triangles, for instance, by simply clicking SELECT at the three points on the screen where you want the corners.

The third icon is similar to the first except that it draws curved lines. Curves are drawn in much the same way as straight lines, but as the second and subsequent lines are drawn, the previous line in each case is bent so as to give the smoothest possible transition into the new direction. Finally, when you click ADJUST to complete your object, control points become visible. Each line entered will display a control point at either end of it. !Draw uses Bezier curves which are very sophisticated digitally defined curved lines. You can "fine tune" your curves to exactly the right shape by holding down ADJUST on the control points and dragging them to the required position. Each control point actually controls two parameters concerning the end of the line to which it relates:

- The first parameter is the direction. The temporary line joining the control point to the curve is a tangent to the curve and shows the direction of the curve at that point. If you change the direction of the temporary line, you are also changing the direction of the curve to which it relates.

- The second parameter is proportion of control. This concept is less easy to grasp. Each curve is of course controlled by two control points, one at each end. The relative lengths of the two temporary lines between the control points and the ends of a curve determine the proportion of the length of the curve that follows the direction set by those control points. The longer the control line the more gradually the curve will change its direction. Figure 5.4 illustrates this.

If this seems hard to grasp, just "play" with the facility for a while. Draw a few really sinuous curved shapes such as outline letter "S"s. You'll soon get the hang of it. Not many DTP systems offer drawing facilities as sophisticated as Bezier curves.

The fourth icon again draws curved lines, but with an auto-close facility.

The fifth icon is for moves. Selecting this allows you to move the pointer without drawing a line, but the move is still recorded as part of the object currently being drawn. It allows an object to consist of more than one continuous sequence of lines. After the "move" the type of line previously selected is automatically reselected.

The sixth and seventh icons are shortcuts for drawing ellipses (including circles) and rectangles (including squares) respectively. Each ellipse or rectangle is a path object in its own right, not a part of another object.

To draw an ellipse or circle, first position the pointer where you wish its centre to be and click SELECT. Next move the pointer to a position on the same longitude and latitude as the outer limits of the ellipse and click SELECT again. Thus, you effectively define the centre and corner of a box which just encloses the ellipse or circle.

To draw a rectangle move the pointer to the point where you want one corner to be and click SELECT. Then move the pointer where you want the diagonally opposite corner to be and click SELECT.

While in any of the above drawing modes, a wide range of styles is available. Click MENU and display the "Style" sub-menu. You can choose your line thickness, line colour and comer pattern (but not on curves or ellipses). There is also a fill colour which by default is "transparent". Only one style parameter can apply to each path object–you cannot for instance have some lines black and some red within the same object.

When the fill colour is transparent, you can of course see other objects behind the transparent object. If, however, you choose a fill colour, the filled object will hide any earlier objects if it overlaps them. Each object is in fact at a definite "height" above the page, later objects being over the top of earlier ones. It's rather like a page layout being made up by pasting items on pieces of paper over the top of existing items and concealing them. But it is possible to change the "height" of objects using SELECT (see above).

Clicking ADJUST with the pointer over a completed path object will take you into "Edit mode". The Edit mode menu allows lines and points in path objects to be moved, deleted and added. Style factors, such as line colour or fill colour can be changed by selecting the object and selecting the required style characteristic via the "Style" sub- menu.

Text Handling in !Draw

The next icon, containing a "T" creates text objects. These will be considered next.

Inevitably this book is largely concerned with text handling in !Draw. One common cause of confusion is that there are two totally different types of object in which !Draw handles text. To add to the confusion their names are very similar. Text objects and text area objects, however, have little in common except that they both display text using the installed font manager and fonts.

Note that while text objects and text area objects can be scaled (scaling works in an unusual manner in text area objects), they cannot be mirrored or inverted and they cannot be rotated.

2. Text Objects

A text object consists of a single line of text which is uniform in style. It can only be created using the text entry facility in !Draw. Click on the "T" icon in the toolbox or "Text" in the "Enter" sub-menu. This places a caret on the screen at the position of the pointer when you next click "select". You can reposition the caret by moving the pointer to a new position and clicking "select". You can now enter text at the keyboard. As you type, the characters appear on the screen at the position of the caret which moves to the right (just as in !Edit). No editing facilities are provided apart from the DELETE key.

At any time while entering a text object you can change any aspect of its "style". Click MENU and display the "Style" sub-menu. You now have a choice of font name, font size, font height, text colour and background colour.

The text background colour is white by default. If you are creating a text object over a background having a different colour, such as a rectangle filled with red, you should set the text background colour to correspond with this background. This is for the purpose of anti- aliasing. If you omit to do this, on the screen display the characters will appear to have faint white outlines. This faint outline, however, does not appear when the page is printed.

At the foot of the "Font size" and "Font height" sub-menus is a "writable" item which by default displays "6.40". You may delete this value and write any value you wish. There are no upper or lower limits and values in decimal fractions of points are permissible, eg 11.25 pt. However, to select it you must remember to click SELECT on it or press RETURN after entering it.

Whenever you select a font size, the font height is automatically set to the same value. You may subsequently select a different value for the font height if you wish. This allows you to alter the aspect of characters, eg to use "condensed" (narrow) or "expanded" (wide) characters.

Note that any changes of style which you make in the course of entering a text object are applied to the characters already in the object–the whole object is rewritten in the newly selected style.

To complete your text object you must press RETURN or click the SELECT button. If you press RETURN the caret now moves to a new position one character height below the start of the object just finished. If you click SELECT, the caret moves to the current pointer position. If you forget to hit RETURN or click SELECT and you enter select mode from the toolbox, the unfinished text object disappears and is lost irretrievably. However, if you click on any other item in the toolbox, the text object will be completed automatically.

You cannot mix styles in one text object. For instance, you cannot have one or two words in italics in the midst of a text object otherwise in roman (i.e., non italic). To create such a line of mixed-style text you must either use a text area object (see below) or use three text objects, one in italics and two in roman, one on either side. These can be moved carefully together and when correctly aligned may be combined into one object by selecting all three and clicking on "Group" in the "Select" menu. When grouped they can be moved and scaled as though they were all one object.

When finished, the contents of a text object can be changed. Select the object and then press CTRL-E and a small window will open with a writable icon containing the text. You can then edit this in the usual RISC OS way. Clicking on "Set" in this window will then alter the text in the actual !Draw window. If you decide not to alter the text just close this window without clicking on "Set".

The contents of a finished text object can also be moved and scaled and its style characteristics can be adjusted. See above on "Select Mode" for more detailed information. Note that when you scale a text object the width and height of the constituent characters are automatically adjusted to fill the new outline. You can easily create very condensed (narrow) or expanded (wide) characters in this way. This makes text objects very useful in DTP for headlines, titles and sub-titles, which can be scaled to fill the space available. They are also useful for other isolated lines of text, for example, figure captions and continuation messages such as "continued on page 5".

If you reload a previously saved !Draw file in which a text object uses a font that has subsequently been deleted from !Fonts, the affected text object will be displayed in the system font. That is, a copy of the font used by the computer in normal screen displays.

3. Text area objects

Text area objects may contain any number of lines of text and the style may be changed as often as you wish. In these features they contrast with text objects.

The text itself must be created in !Edit or another text editor such as !StrongED or !Zap as a normal text file. Attempts to load text files from word processors have no effect. The text file should contain a special header similar to the one described in Chapter 6. If it lacks such a header, a default header is substituted. The text file must conclude with a carriage return.

The text can be transferred from !Edit to !Draw directly if both !Edit and !Draw windows are open simultaneously. Save the !Edit text file in the normal way, but instead of dragging the icon into a directory viewer, drag it into the !Draw window. Alternatively if the text file has been saved to disc, drag its icon from the directory viewer into the !Draw window. If no !Draw window is open, drag the text file icon on to the !Draw icon on the icon bar.

If the file transfer is successful, the text area at first appears in the !Draw window as a standard-sized "block" (measuring 1.5 x 1.5 inches on the grid) or as several such blocks side by side if the header specified more than one column. Most users are at first horrified to find that only the first few words of their text are present and they fear that the bulk of their text has fallen into the computer equivalent of a black hole. Don't panic! It's all there, even though much of it is invisible.

The text area can be moved and scaled using the select facility. Moving works in exactly the same way as for other objects, but scaling works differently. The character size and line spacing cannot be changed in !Draw; these are fixed by the contents of the text file and can only be altered by modifying the text file (in !Edit) and transferring it back into !Draw. The size and shape of the text area can be changed as you wish by the normal scaling procedure. Each time you change its shape the text rearranges itself automatically to fill the text area. As you make the area bigger, more of the text, which at first seemed to be missing, appears. When the text area is big enough, all of the text appears.

If your header requested more than one column, the text will at first appear in a number of standard-sized boxes side by side, their number being the number of columns that your header specified. When you first click SELECT on the text area, the entire text area is selected, one dotted red boundary box embracing all the columns. You should now click SELECT again on the first column; that column alone will be selected and outlined. This can now be moved and scaled as before. As you change its size, the text will rearrange itself right through all the subsequent columns. This is illustrated in Figure 5.5.

Personally, I find the term "columns" misleading–it conjures up images of equal-width columns in newspapers and telephone directories. I prefer to think of them as "text boxes". Certainly they can be parallel and given equal widths, if that is what the layout demands, but in practice there is no restriction on the number of them (apart from a maximum of 99), nor on their sizes or relative positions. This means that by using an assortment of different-sized boxes you can wrap text around illustrations just as in proper DTP systems!

If you spot a spelling or style mistake in a text area object, you have no choice but to return to .'Edit, reload the text file if necessary, and make the corrections there. You can then transfer the corrected text file back to !Draw. If you drag the icon over the existing text area, the amended text will replace the previous version, so the error will disappear. If you did not save the original text file (if, for instance, you transferred it straight from '.Edit to /Draw and then quit !Edit), all is not lost. Select the text area in /Draw, click "menu", obtain the "Save" sub-menu and one of the options will allow you to save the text area as an !Eait-style text file.

Clicking SELECT once on the text causes the whole text area to be selected, (b) Clicking SELECT twice over a text column causes that column alone to be selected, (c) The selected column can now be moved and scaled, the text reformatting itself throughout the columns.

4. Sprites

Sprites can be imported into !Draw by "dragging" the sprite file icon into the !Draw window. Once in !Draw they can be moved, scaled, inverted or mirrored, but not rotated. They are considered in more detail in Chapter 9.

6 : Creating the text

The Header and \ Commands

The text area file for !Draw which you create using !Edit is not quite like any other text file. Special formatting commands can be inserted; these are all introduced with the backslash character "\". In addition, the text file must begin with a special header sequence. If this is omitted, !Draw may ignore the file altogether, generate an error message or substitute a default header. The header must begin with the line:

    \! 1

The space is optional. The number, called the version number, must be 1 otherwise an error message will be generated when the file is transferred to !Draw.

The header typically contains details of the fonts to be used, their sizes, line spacing, margins, alignment, the number of columns or boxes and the text and background colours. Most of these effects have default values. This means that, if you do not define them, the software will itself choose a value.

If a text file lacking a version number line is imported into !Draw, the following "default header" is attached to the text:

    \! 1
    \F 0 Trinity .Medium 12
    \F 1 Corpus-Medium 12
    \0
    \AD
    \L12

This defines Font 0 as 12 pt Trinity Medium, Font 1 as 12 pt Corpus Medium, selects Font 0 as the current font and sets the line spacing to 12 pt with "double justification", ie both left- and right-hand edges to be straight.

The full list of "\" commands is as follows. Note that all commands are case sensitive so you cannot use lower-case letters in place of capitals as this will cause errors. Most commands must be terminated by a <CR> or a slash (/), but some, particularly font-change commands, need no termination unless it is necessary to avoid ambiguity.

\!   Version line

This line must begin your text file or the default header will be substituted. The \! must be followed by the version number which must be 1. The command must be terminated by a / or a <CR>. For example:

    \!1

\A   Alignment

The \A must be followed immediately by one of the following: L (left); R (right); C (centred) or D (double). The command may be terminated by a /, but this is optional. For example:

    \AD

This causes following text to be printed with double alignment.

Left alignment means that the left margin is straight, but the right margin is ragged, as in conventional typing.

Right alignment means that the right margin is straight, but the left margin is ragged. This effect is useful for certain display purposes and also in letter headings.

Centred alignment means that the text is centred between the margins. This is useful in titles, sub-titles, letter headings and other forms of display.

Double alignment means that the text has both left and right margins straight as in most books, newspapers and magazines. The spaces between words are evenly expanded to bring lines to the full width.

\B Set background colour

The B must be followed by three numbers between 0 and 255, separated by spaces. The numbers represent the proportions of red, green and blue respectively in the new background colour. Values greater than 255 are treated as 255 and values less than 0 are treated as 0. The command must be terminated by a <CR> or a /. For example:

\B0 0 0/

This sets the background colour to black.

The default is:

\B255 255 255/

This sets the background colour to white.

Note that changes to the background colour are not effective unless the specified colour is already present in the area. Also a "bug" in the printer driver software may cause problems in printing text areas that are not in the default colours.

\C Set text colour

The C must be followed by three numbers between 0 and 255, separated by spaces. The numbers represent the proportions of red, green and blue respectively in the new text colour. Values greater than 255 are treated as 255 and values less than 0 are treated as 0. The command must be terminated by a <CR> or a /. For example:

\C255 255 255/

This sets the text colour to white.

The default is:

\C0 0 0/

This sets the text colour to black.

\D Set number of columns or boxes

D must be followed by a number in the range 1 to 99 and the command must be terminated by a <CR> or a /. The default number is 1. The command must appear before any text is printed. For example:

\D 6

This would cause the text to appear in six columns or boxes which subsequently can be re-sized and rearranged to suit the layout of the document.

\F   Define font

The F must be followed by a font number (any number in the range 0 to 99), then by the filename for the font to be allocated that number, then by the font size in points. Optionally the font width may be defined after the font size; if omitted it is set to the same value as the font size. Spaces are compulsory between all items in the command except between the \F and the font number. The command must be terminated by a / or a <CR>. For example:

\F0 Trinity.Medium 12
\F1 Trinity.Medium.Italic 12
\F2 Trinity.Bold.Italic 12
\F10 Trinity.Medium 9
\F99 Trinity.Bold 12 16

This sequence of commands defines five fonts from the Trinity family. Normally these definitions will be in the header. In this document the appearance of text will depend on the preceding symbol as follows:

Symbol	Following text
\0	12 pt Trinity Medium
\1	12 pt Trinity Medium Italic
\2	12 pt Trinity Bold Italic
\10	9 pt Trinity Medium
\99	Extended 12 pt Trinity Bold

Extended text has an extra bold appearance.

As can be seen, font numbers need not be assigned sequentially. If the same font is to be used in two different sizes (like Trinity Medium in the example), a separate definition is needed for each size.

When the text file is transferred into !Draw, the program will attempt to ensure that the specified fonts are present in the ! Fonts directory. If any of the specified fonts are not present, an error message ("Unable to Load Font <filename>") is given, and another font, usually the one previously used, is substituted.

\L   Set line spacing

The \L must be followed by a number; a space is optional between the \L and the number. The command must be terminated by a <CR> or a /.

The number is the line spacing in points. This is the distance from the base of the characters in the current line to the base of the characters in the next line. For example:

\L 12/

This sets (or changes) the line spacing to 12 pt 1/6 inch). The command often appears in the header, but it need not do so. If omitted, a default line spacing of 10 pt is applied. You may also use the command at any point in the text where you wish to change the line spacing. The change of spacing takes effect from the end of the line (in the !Draw text area) in which the command falls.

\M   Set margins

The \M must be followed by two numbers separated by a space. A space is optional between the \M and the first number. The command must be terminated by a <CR> or a /.

The command sets or changes the margins, ie the space between the edges of the column or box (as revealed using the 'select' facility in !Draw) and the text itself. The first number is the left margin in points and the second number is the right margin in points. The new margin settings apply immediately if executed at the beginning of a line. Otherwise they apply from the end of the line in which the command appears. By default both margins are 1 pt. For example:

\M36 1/

This sets the new left margin to 36 pt (1/2 inch) and the right margin to 1 pt. The command is useful for applying temporary indents in text areas.

Note that it is possible to make the margins so large that they meet or overlap, squeezing out the text altogether. This does not cause an error, but it does prevent the text from appearing.

\P   Set paragraph spacing

The \P must be followed by a number; a space is optional between the \P and the number. The command must be terminated by a <CR> or a /.

The number is the spacing in points that will be inserted between paragraphs. For example:

\P 24/

This sets the space between paragraphs to 24 pt (1/3 in). To create a new paragraph in a text file press <CR> twice. On the !Edit screen this starts two new lines, so that a blank line appears between paragraphs. In the text area in !Draw the blank line will be replaced by a space having the value set. If the value is the same as the current line spacing, a blank line of standard spacing will appear between paragraphs. If the value is 0 no extra space will be inserted between the paragraphs; the new paragraph will start immediately below the previous one. A value equal to half the current line spacing gives an effect that many find pleasing–it separates paragraphs by half a line space.

The command often appears in headers, but need not do so. If omitted, a default value of 10 pt is assumed. The command may be inserted at any point in the text file where you wish to change the amount of space between paragraphs. The new value takes effect at the end of the paragraph in which it is placed. This can be very useful if you wish to space out the paragraphs so that they exactly fill adjacent columns. Note that you may also create new paragraphs having no intervening space by terminating the paragraph with \<CR>. This simply forces a new line. The effect is exactly the same as <CR><CR> after a \PO/ command. A single <CR> (not preceded by \) is treated by !Draw as a space (for reasons that are explained later).

\U   Underline

The \U is followed by the underline position (a number in the range - 128 to 127) and the underline thickness (a number in the range 0 to 255). A space is compulsory between the two numbers and optional between the \U and the underline position. The command must be terminated by a / or a <CR>. Both numbers are in units of ^{1}/256th of the current font size. For example:

\U -128 26/

This turns on underlining of 1 pt thickness (a 10 pt font is assumed) at the lowest possible position, which on most fonts is well below the tips of the descenders. In general a position setting of about -70 looks good. Aim for a thickness of about 1 pt.

If the position number is set to 127, this sets the underline position to about half a font height above the base line, at about the same level as the tops of lower case characters such as c and n. So unfortunately, this facility cannot be used to insert bars above words and symbols as used in describing logic functions.

To turn underlining off, either set a new underline having thickness 0, or, more conveniently, issue the following:

\U.

The shorthand command \U. may be terminated with a / but this is not strictly necessary.

\V   Vertical move

\V must be followed by a single-digit number in the range -9 to 9. A space is optional between the \V and the number. The command must be terminated by a / or a <CR>. The number is the number of points by which the following text must be moved upwards. Negative numbers, of course, move the text downwards.

The purpose of this command is to allow the inclusion of subscript and superscript characters. These will normally need to be in a font approximately half the size of the one in general use. For example:

H\V-4/\1/2\V4/\0O

will print H20 assuming that the current font is a 12 pt font assigned to font 0 and font 1 is same font in 6 pt size.

If you wish to use superscript or subscript figures 1, 2 and 3, note that there is a simple way to do so. The Acorn outline fonts include superscript figures 1, 2 and 3 in ASCII codes 185, 178 and 179 respectively. These can be selected in the normal way. To convert them to subscript simply use a \V command to lower the printing position by a suitable amount (roughly half the font size).

After issuing a \V command, remember to issue another \V command having the same value but of opposite sign to restore printing to its normal level.

\<CR>   Start new line

This forces the start of a new line. An isolated <CR> is regarded as equivalent to a space. To start a paragraph you are recommended to press <CR> twice. This starts a new line and inserts before it the space set by the \P command.

\-   Soft hyphen

!Draw normally only splits lines at spaces. You may, however, insert \- into a long word, which indicates to !Draw that it may split the word at this position, inserting a hyphen, if it needs to. If it does not need to, the command has no effect.

\ [font number]   Change font

The font number must be a number between 0 and 99 and must follow the \ without any intervening space. The font number must have been assigned to a font using a \F command earlier in the text. The command may be terminated by a / but this is not strictly necessary. However, it is advisable to insert the . it the text character immediately following it is a number.

This command may be issued at any point in the text where a change of font is required, such as a change from roman to italic characters or a change to a smaller font for superscript or subscript printing.

    \\   Insert \ character

Since the \ character is used to identify embedded commands, this special provision has been made for those occasions when you may wish to actually print a backslash in your document.

    \; Comment

This allows you to write comments in your text file. The comments will appear on screen in '.Edit, but will not appear on screen in !Draw text areas or in printouts. All text following \; up to the next <CR> is regarded as comment.

This facility, which is equivalent to REM in BASIC program listings, is most useful for reminding yourself of the purpose of some piece of text.

Paragraphs and <CR> Characters

Unless you deliberately set your text editor to format the text there will normally be no <CR> characters in the text except where you have pressed the RETURN key. Since the lines of text on the screen in !Edit are likely to be broken in different places from those in the text area in !Draw, it is clear that <CR> cannot have its normal new line effect in !Draw.

The rules concerning the way !Draw treats <CR> characters in text areas are as follows:

- An isolated <CR> is treated as a space.
- A <CR> preceded by a space or followed by a space is ignored.
- A <CR> preceded by a \ forces a new line.
- Two <CR>s in sequence start a new paragraph separated by the space specified in the last issued \P command; if no \P has been issued the default space of 10 pt is applied.
- A sequence of n <CR> characters inserts n-1 paragraph spacings.
- Paragraph spacings at the start of the text are ignored.

7 : The Font System

Outline Fonts and Bitmap Fonts.

The original fonts supplied with the Archimedes and A3000 computers were bitmap fonts. This means that the shapes of the characters were stored as numbers which represented the colours of the individual dots that made up each character's image. Bitmaps were provided for several different sizes of font. Sizes not included were obtained by enlarging or reducing the nearest available size. Not surprisingly, for very large font sizes this gave a hideously crude appearance. However, with the almost universal use of the Acorn outline font manager text should always appear smooth, even in very large point sizes, unless you have deliberately chosen to ue a bitmap font.

Fonts are required for two quite distinct processes. They appear on the monitor screen in an accurate representation of the page being designed and they are sent as graphics to the printer when the page is printed. The two requirements are quite different. The screen has far coarser resolution than most printers–even a Mode 20 multisync screen has only 640 pixels (dots) from edge to edge, whereas an Epson FX-80 or compatible dot-matrix printer can print a nominal 1920 dots across a page of A4. The screen, however, has one advantage over the printer–it can display intermediate shades. The printer can only put dots of one colour, most often black, on the paper, which is usually white.

Anti-aliasing

The ability of the screen to display intermediate shades led to one of the most advanced features of the Archimedes and A3000 computers–the use of "anti-aliased" character displays.

When displaying a complex shape using a fairly coarse medium such as the matrix of pixels on a monitor screen, it is inevitable that there will be inaccuracies. Consider, for instance, the problems involved in displaying a large black letter "A" against a white background. Some pixels will be wholly in areas covered by the black strokes of the character. Clearly these pixels will be "off" so they appear black. Some pixels will be wholly in areas not touched by the strokes of the character; for instance, in the hollows in the centre of the character. Clearly these will be "on" and therefore white. But many pixels will be in areas partially covered by the strokes of the character, especially as the two main strokes of this character are at angles. If the monitor display were confined to black and white, clearly pixels along the edges of these angled strokes would introduce irregularities into the shape of the character as seen on the screen. The angled lines would not appear straight, but would rise in steps as shown below. This is known as "aliasing".

There is, however, a solution to this problem. That is to show the partially obscured pixels in intermediate shades of grey. A pixel representing an area that is largely covered by a stroke displays a dark shade, while a pixel that is only slightly obscured displays a lighter shade. The edges of the letter "A" now appear to be straight. In fact this is an illusion; magnify the screen display, as in Figure 7.2, and you will see that the edges of the "A" are still far from straight, but the grey shades form a visual buffer between the black and white areas of the screen making the aliasing far less obvious. This process is called anti-aliasing and it gives the appearance of resolution well in excess of the monitor's capability.

Unfortunately, anti-aliasing is no help to the printer since the printer cannot handle intermediate shades. This is why printouts from applications using bitmapped fonts always appear somewhat crude.

Outline Fonts

The introduction of the Acorn outline font system, however, led to dramatic improvements in both screen and printout quality. Outline fonts are created using a font editor application, !FontEd, in which the outline of each character is drawn using routines similar to the path object drawing routines in !Draw. The computer records the plotting instructions for each character and stores them in a file called *Outlines*. Another file called *IntMetrics* stores data concerning each character's width and height.

The principal advantage of this system is that it is totally independent of font size. Any size of font can be specified and the computer will simply multiply the plot distances by the requested font size resulting in perfectly formed characters of that size, both on screen and on paper. It is even possible to specify different font sizes for height and width so that *condensed* (narrower than natural) or *expanded* (wider than natural) characters are produced.

When putting characters on the screen, the font manager software first plots the character on a "virtual" screen to produce a fully anti-aliased bitmap of the character at the requested size. This is then copied to the screen. As characters are used, so their bitmaps are stored in a reserved area of memory called the font cache. Use of a font cache greatly speeds up the rate at which characters can be put on the screen. Without it, the software would need to access the disc repeatedly for plotting instructions and repeat the outline-to-bitmap conversion for each occurrence of a character. Hence writing on the screen would become painfully slow.

When printing on paper the character plotting instructions are converted to another bitmap – this time, of course, without anti-aliasing. However, the resolution used is generally much higher, appropriate to the graphics mode selected on the printer driver. Even low-cost 9-pin dot-matrix printers which support graphics at 240 x 216 dots per inch are capable of giving finely detailed, impressive printouts.

How Outline Fonts are Organised

As mentioned above, each outline font consists of two files, one named Outlines and one named IntMetrics. The organisation of font files uses, to excellent advantage, the hierarchical directory-within-directory structure of the Acorn Advanced Disc Filing System.

Outline fonts are normally stored in the application directory called !Fonts which also contains two modules concerned with font management. Any fonts not included in !Fonts will not be recognised as fonts bv the font manager.

Let us consider the collection of fonts in the Acorn Font Starter package. This includes three 'families' of fonts; Corpus, Homerton and Trinity. Cataloguing !Fonts will reveal that Corpus, Homerton and Trinity are three directories. Let us concentrate on Trinity. Cataloguing Trinity will show that it contains two further directories named Bold and Medium. Catalogue either of these and you will find that the contents consist of two font files which, as we should expect, are named IntMetrics and Outlines. Each also contains a further directory named Italic, itself containing two font files, IntMetrics and Outlines.

This structure is summarised in Figure 7.3. This accounts for the four fonts in the Trinity "family":

Trinity.Bold

Trinity.Bold.Italic

Trinity.Medium

Trinity.Medium.Italic

Exactly the same pattern applies to Corpus and Homerton, except that the Italic variants are described as "Oblique" and this is reflected in the names of the appropriate directories

Renaming Fonts

You cannot rename fonts by simply changing the names of the directories in which they are stored. Each "Outlines" file and each "IntMetrics" file contains the full path name below !Fonts and a note is made of this whenever the font manager accesses a file. Suppose, for instance, you renamed the Trinity" directory "Times", and then from !Draw you attempted to create a text object in, say. Times Medium. Then for each character the font would be reloaded from disc, a tediously slow process! This is because the font cache registers the name stored internally in the font file and so regards the font it loaded as Trinity Medium, not Times Medium. To rename a font, in addition to renaming the directories, you must change the pathname entry in the Outlines and IntMetrics files. To do this you must load the font into the Font Editor application, make the necessary changes in its "change" option, and then resave the amended files into the appropriate directories.

Handling Large Collections of Fonts

Outline fonts are available from several sources and you may in time find yourself amassing a considerable collection of them. Since a font can only be used if it is located in the !Fonts application directory, you may quickly find yourself facing a problem. A typical Outlines file is 20 to 30 Kilobytes long, its attendant IntMetrics file 2 to 3 Kilobytes long and each directory is 2 Kilobytes long. So a single font "family" with four variations such as Homerton or Trinity takes up about 120 Kilobytes.

In theory you can place about 70 new font directories in !Fonts, allowing 70 font families. Unfortunately, it's not as simple as that. Some applications can crash if you have too many fonts, and overlarge font menus can become extremely awkward and cumbersome in use.

The easiest solution is to use a Font Manager program which enables you to "switch" fonts in and out of use but if you don't want to do this you could store all your fonts in an innocuously named directory such as *Fontstore* and keep a much smaller number in !Fonts. In !Fonts I keep the fonts I use most frequently, a total of about 30, plus a number of "visiting" fonts copied across for special purposes. This "visiting" population is perpetually changing.

Varieties of Typeface

One of the joys of DTP is that, as you create a document, you are offered a choice of typefaces. You are no longer restricted to the single style, size and weight of your typewriter typeface or even to the broader but still limited choice offered by most dot-matrix printers.

There are many kinds of typeface and you can use any for any purpose, but nevertheless most are more suitable for certain types of job than others. Let us briefly examine the five font families in the current Acorn and Beebug Font Packs as they are representative of three quite contrasting kinds of typeface.

Corpus is a typewriter-style typeface based on a design named Courier. As on an old-fashioned typewriter, it is a fixed-width face, that is, all characters have the same width, irrespective of their designs. In this, Corpus stands in contrast with Homerton and Trinity which are proportionally spaced, ie the widths of the characters vary according to their designs–a "W" being clearly rather wider than an "\"".

Corpus is best suited to certain specialised tasks. If you are creating a user manual for a piece of software. Corpus would be suitable for representing input to and output from the computer, since most normal computer displays and printouts are similarly fixed-width. Or if you are designing pages for a magazine or newsletter and you wish to reproduce a letter and to emphasise that it is a letter, put it in Corpus while the rest of publication is in Trinity or Homerton. This will make the letter stand out from the surrounding items and its typescript-like appearance will lend it an air of urgency–as though it had arrived late but was so important that you decided to publish it without typesetting it!

Homerton and **SwissB** from Beebug are sans-serif typefaces based on a popular design called Helvetica (or Swiss). Sans-serif means that it lacks the serifs or protrusions at the ends of strokes that are so characteristic of typefaces like Trinity and Corpus. A distinctive feature of Helvetica and its derivatives is that all lines are equal in width. Consequently, if you compress Homerton, the vertical strokes get narrower while the horizontal ones remain unchanged and the result does not look right. If you expand Homerton, the vertical strokes get broader, which also does not look right, although the effect is not so disturbing as the condensed effect. This is shown below.

This in normal 20 point Homerton Medium

This in normal 20 point Homerton Medium condensed to 75%

This is the same font expanded to 125%

Helvetica-style typefaces are used for a very wide range of purpose including the text of news items and articles in some magazines. They are not ideally suited for this, however, since their legibility is not ai good as some other typefaces. They are better suited to titles, sub titles, introductory paragraphs and advertisement displays.

Trinity is based on **Times**, named after the newspaper in which it originated. It is a formal serif face offering very high legibility and is therefore ideal for large masses of text in newspapers, magazine articles and books. Its strokes are of varying widths, verticals being generally broader than horizontals. This means that it can be readily expanded or compressed without losing its essential character or sacrificing its legibility.

Paladin in the Beebug font pack is a serif typeface like Trinity, but with a totally different "feel". It is based on a typeface called Palatine influenced as its name suggests by the "chancery cursive" used by scribes in Venice and Rome in the 15th and 16th centuries. Its complex curves give it an air of elegance or even fussiness. It is ideal fo documentation that needs an up-market air such as catalogue; brochures, stylish magazines and some kinds of book.

Vogue in the Beebug font pack is a sans-serif face which offers dramatic contrast from the Helvetica family. Based on a design called *Avant-Garde,* it is a geometrically proportioned typeface compose mainly from circles and straight lines. It originated in the 1930s and i redolent of the "Art Deco" design fashions of that period. It is nc really suitable for textual work, but is eminently suitable for creating fashionable displays.

Recently Beebug has released some additional fonts. Besides a Courier-equivalent, **Bookmark** is a formal serif font with a more spacious feel than Trinity. Based on Bookman which was originally intended for use in headings, it is ideally suited to a wide range of text and display work. **Chaucer**, offered in Medium italic only, is, like Palatine, derived from Chancery Cursive and is inspired by a font called Zapf Chancery. Its antique appearance lends it to specialist design and display work.

The Character Set

The Latin alphabets used in Acorn outline fonts conform to a standard known as ISO 8859/1. This follows the standard ASCII 7-bit character set for codes 32 to 127 but it also uses the further 128 8-bit codes from 128 to 255. This allows the inclusion of many other useful characters and symbols besides sufficient accented characters to cater for most European languages. The complete character set of Trinity Medium is given in Appendix 1.

ISO 8859/1 leaves codes 128 to 159 undefined (allowing the user to define his own characters in these codes) but in practice the Acorn and Beebug fonts have introduced some useful additional characters into codes 143 to 159. These are:

143	•	"bullet"
144	'	open single quote
145	'	close single quote or apostrophe
146	‹	open French single quote
147	›	close French single quote
148	"	open double quotes
149	"	close double quotes
150	„	ditto mark
151	–	en-dash
152	—	em-dash
153	–	minus sign
154	Œ	capital OE diphthong
155	œ	lower-case oe diphthong
156	†	dagger
157	‡	double dagger
158	fi	fi ligature
159	fl	fl ligature
164	€	Euro symbol
169	©	Copyright symbol
174	®	Registered trade mark
176	°	Degree symbol
177	±	Plus or Minus symbol

Characters 128 to 142 are still undefined and so their codes are available for user-defined characters. To define new characters you will need the Acorn !FontEd application.

Normally the keyboard only allows access to characters having codes in the region 32 to 127. So how can you use characters having codes above 127? There are two ways.

Some, but not all, codes can be accessed direct from the keyboard using special combinations of keys:

160	NBSP	Alt + space
162	¢	Alt+C
165	¥	Alt + Y
167	§	Alt + S
171	«	Alt + Z
173	-	Alt + -
178	²	Alt + 2
179	³	Alt + 3
181	µ	Alt + M
185	¹	Alt + 1
187	»	Alt + X

Note that in many instances the alternative character is similar to the one obtained by pressing the key without Alt.

The alternative way of obtaining any character is to hold down the Alt key, enter the decimal code of the required character on the numeric keypad and then release the Alt key. For example, to obtain open double quotes in !Draw or !Edit, hold down Alt, enter 148 on the numeric keypad and then release Alt. In !Edit you may find that the wrong character appears on the screen–don't worry, it will be replaced by the right one when the file is transferred to !Draw.

The facility whereby non-keyboard characters can be accessed using combinations of the function keys with Shift or Ctrl or both is unfortunately not available in !Draw or !Edit. Character 160 is described as "NBSP" which stands for "Non-Break Space". It is a space, the same width as the standard space (character 32). It differs from the standard space, however, in that it behaves as a normal character rather than as a delimiter between words. Both !Edit and !Draw will break lines at a standard space, but not at a NBSP, hence its name. So it is useful where you wish two words to remain together on the same line. It is also useful in that its width is constant, whereas that of the standard space can in some circumstances be varied, as, for instance, in justified text. If you require a fixed-width space, eg in paragraph indentations or in columns of figures, use NBSP in preference to the standard space.

In proportionally spaced fonts such as Trinity, the figures all have the same width to facilitate their tidy arrangement in columns and tables. The width of the space and NBSP is equal to half that of a figure, so to substitute spaces for absent figures, allow two spaces per figure.

8: Page Layout

Before you can begin to think about the design of a page, you must consider the overall document size, page size and the number of pages the document needs.

Multi-Page Documents

One frequent complaint about !Draw as a DTP system is that it does not allow the creation of multi-page documents. In a sense that is true–each !Draw window contains only one "page". Although you can have several !Draw windows open simultaneously, you cannot divide a text area between them (although you can transfer the same text file into all of them).

There is, however, a simple way in which multi-page documents can be handled. The "paper limits" sub-menu in the "miscellaneous" menu in !Draw allows you to select page sizes ranging from A5 to A0 with A4 as the default. You may deliberately choose a larger page size than the one you are using and divide it into page-sized portions. For example, if you are laying out a magazine article consisting of four pages of A4, you may select A2 and draw guide lines vertically and horizontally through the centre of the sheet. You have now divided your A2 sheet into four A4-sized areas which you may treat as pages. You may place your text area boxes wherever you wish on these "pages" since !Draw regards them all as one large page.

Printing such a "multi-page document" demands care. If your printer handles only A4-sized pages, the printable area revealed by selecting "Show" on the "Paper limits" sub-menu (if the printer driver is or has been installed) will be in the bottom left-hand quarter of the sheet. Print this page first. You may delete the "page divider" lines if you wish, but they will probably be just outside the printable area shown by the paper limits, and so not matter. Although the printable area itself cannot be moved, the contents of the sheet can be moved relative to it, which amounts to much the same thing. On the "Select" sub- menu choose "Select all". You can now drag the entire contents of the sheet until another of your A4 pages fits snugly in the printable area and then print it. Repeat this process until all the pages have been printed.

Theoretically there is nothing, apart from memory availability, to prevent you from choosing an A0 sheet size and dividing this into 16 pages of A4 or even 32 of A5. But, as always, there is a price to pay for this facility. The more contents you have on your sheet, the slower the scrolling and printing becomes–especially the printing! Before each pass of the printer head all of the objects have to be examined to see how they affect the portion of the page about to be printed. By all means use this "multi-page" capability, but in moderation.

Page Layouts

Having decided the page size and the number of pages needed, you can turn to the layout of individual pages. Obviously this is to some extent a subjective matter–"if it looks good, it is good". Detailed consideration of the artistic principles behind page layout are out of place in this book. You will find plenty of expert guidance in books on print and design in your local public library. There are, however, some fundamentals that can be briefly outlined.

Probably the page size that you will use most often is A4. This is the most popular paper size in Europe and it is the default page size in !Draw.

Your layout will be influenced by the nature of the document. If it is a poster advertising a meeting, of necessity it needs to attract attention from a distance and so the type sizes must be large; say from 24 to 150 pt. All lines will in theory be the full width of the page, excluding the margins.

Columns

If, on the other hand, it is a page of a magazine article, you will need much smaller typefaces. The main bulk of the article, the "body text", will probably use type in the size range 8 to 12 pt. The main title might be as large as 24 or 36 pt. Intermediate sizes would be used for sub titles. But if you choose, say, 8 pt Trinity Medium for your body text, readers will find the article difficult to read if the lines run right across the page. This is why magazine pages, like newspapers, are generally laid out in columns. An A4 page is often divided into two columns each 20 or 21 ems wide (one em is 1/6 in or 12 pt) or three columns each 13 or 14 ems wide. A news page consisting of mainly short items might use four columns each 9.5 or 10 ems wide. Typically gaps about 1 em wide are left between the columns.

Leading

You will also need to consider the amount of space between adjacent lines of body text. This is known as the "leading", a term which dates from the days when printers inserted thin strips of type metal (a tin/lead alloy) between adjacent lines of type to space them out. Leading makes columns easier to read because it helps the eyes to find their way from the end of one line to the start of the next. The wider the columns the more leading they need. In practice the outline fonts have considerable in-built leading to allow space for accents on capital letters. So, if you set the line spacing to the same value as the font height, the text will look quite acceptable in narrow columns. But with wider columns make the line spacing 1,2 or even 3 points greater than the font height.

Style sheets

If you are using !Draw and !Edit to produce a magazine, you will want to give it consistency by ensuring that the columns are of uniform width and height on all the pages. In the olden days of cut and paste this was done using "make-up sheets" on which the columns were accurately ruled out. The galley proofs were cut up and pasted following these column guides. The DTP equivalent of this is a blank style page, that is a page which has guide lines for the columns and margins already in place. Most DTP packages allow you to set up standard style pages.

As usual you can do this in !Draw. Set up a blank page of the correct size and orientation. From the main menu display the "Grid" sub- menu and then select "show". I still think in ems, a legacy of my background in trade journalism. Therefore I find it easiest to change the grid subdivisions to six per inch, each equal to one em. However, you may feel happier with other units. Turn on "Grid Lock" and mark out your columns using brightly coloured rectangles, I prefer bright green. They will automatically snap to the grid so it's easy to ensure they are all uniform size and correctly positioned. Some people also like to have horizontal rules across the page dividing it into, say, quarters. You can add these using !Draw's "line" facility if you wish. When you transfer your text in from !Edit, simply manipulate the text boxes or columns until their red outlines coincide with the column guides. But, unlike the page dividers mentioned above, you must remember to delete them before printing or the printer will faithfully reproduce them as dotted lines. If you "Group" ("Select" sub-menu) all the column guides and other guide lines they can all be deleted in one fell swoop.

Most magazine pages have running footlines, typically with the magazine title on each left-hand page and the issue date on each right- hand page. These can be inserted on to the style page as text objects; you will of course need separate left-hand and right-hand style pages unless you work your pages in pairs. You must remember to update the date line each issue. Once the style pages are made up, save them. Then you can reload them each time you wish to start work on a fresh page. But rename and resave the page immediately or else there is a real danger that you will resave your finished or half-finished page with the style page file name, deleting your precious style page!

How To Create Some Special Effects

Tables

!Draw itself has no tabulator. But, as usual, there are several ways to create tables in !Edit!Draw. Each presents its own peculiar advantages and disadvantages.

- Create it as a set of text objects in !Draw, each individual item in the table being a separate text object. All can be manipulated carefully to the right places. Using "Grid Lock" will help you to get items correctly aligned. This method is probably the easiest to understand, but it is fiddly and not elegant.

- Create it "horizontally" in '.Edit as a text area object or part of a text area object, using !Edit's tabulator. This is probably the most straightforward method, but it has one massive disadvantage. In proportionally spaced fonts such as Trinity and Homerton the spaces used by the tabulator do not correspond to character widths since the characters have various widths. Any attempt to create a table using this method and a proportionally-spaced font will result in an appalling mess! For this reason you are confined to using fixed-width fonts such as Corpus and your table will look as though it has been created using a typewriter. Figures 8.3a and 8.3b show what happens when you create a table by this method using Trinity and Corpus respectively.

- Create it "vertically" in !Edit as a text area object or part of a text area object. This requires you to think "columns" instead of "lines". In the header allow enough columns (\D) to compose your table column by column. When you type the contents, work down each column, ending each entry with \<CR>, in turn. When you transfer the file to !Edit, arrange that each column's contents form a separate column and move the resulting columns until they line up neatly. Once you've mastered thinking "vertically" this method is very easy and does give neat results with proportional fonts. (c) in the illustration below shows a table created in this way.

Your contact details are as follows:

(a)

General enquiries	Jane Smith	ext 4904
Sales	Peter Evans	ext 4908
Servicing	Tom Jones	ext 4916
Accounts	John Brown	ext 4911

(b)

```
Your contact details are as follows:

General enquiries   Jane Smith    ext 4904
Sales               Peter Evans   ext 4908
Servicing           Tom Jones     ext 4916
Accounts            John Brown    ext 4911
```

(c)

Your contact details are as follows:

General enquiries	Jane Smith	ext 4904
Sales	Peter Evans	ext 4908
Servicing	Tom Jones	ext 4916
Accounts	John Brown	ext 4911

The illustration above shows three methods of producing a table. The "horizontal method" using !Edit's tabulator gives untidy results using proportionally spaced fonts such as Trinity (a). It is tidier with fixed width fonts such as Corpus (b), but would look much better using the "vertical" method shown in (c).

With tables containing numbers do remember that numbers need to be aligned by their least significant figure. This means that if you are working with numbers having varying lengths you must add leading spaces before shorter numbers to make them up to the length of the longest. And in proportionally spaced fonts two spaces will be required to compensate for each missing digit. For example, a column containing the numbers 8, 115, 27 and 1066 looks wrong if printed thus:

8
115
27

    1066

But with leading spaces added the columns line up correctly:

      8
    115
    27
    1066

Drawings

One significant advantage of !Draw over most "real" DTP packages lies in its comprehensive graphics tools. Its extensive drawing facilities were briefly described in Chapter 5 and are explained in depth in the User Manual. It also allows you to import sprites such as saved screens, parts of saved screens, clip art and any sprites which you have created in !Paint. These are considered in more detail in the next chapter.

!Draw's facility for drawing lines, boxes and geometrical shapes with or without fill colours provides a very powerful tool for DTP work. It allows you to create the graphs, bar charts and pie charts which are often used in reports, presentations and technical articles. Pie charts and bar charts are considered in detail below. Labels and lettering can easily be inserted as text objects. Finally grouping all the components of the diagram allows you to scale the entire item to fit the space available on the page.

Drop shadows

Drop shadows are a most attractive effect. A drop shadow is an apparent shadow, normally in black or grey, behind an item in a box, whether a heading or news item or illustration or announcement. By creating the illusion that the box is "floating" in space a little in front of the page and casting a shadow on to it, it helps to attract the reader's attention. Drop shadows are straightforward to create if you think through the steps logically. There are several methods and the following, though arguably clumsy, is easy to follow and works well enough.

Making a
DROP
SHADOW
Display box

Stage 1

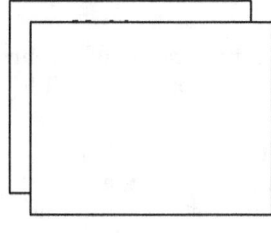

Making a
DROP
SHADOW
Display box

Stage 2

Stage 3

Making a
DROP
SHADOW
Display box

Stage 4

- First compose the text, logo, diagram or other content that is to go inside the box having the shadow.

- Then select the "rectangle" icon. Click MENU and display the "Style" sub-menu. Choose your line width and colour and also your fill colour, that is the background colour for the box which will most probably be white. Do not leave the fill colour as the default "transparent". Now "pull out" a box around its contents. When the box is finished its fill colour will of course conceal the contents, since later objects obscure earlier ones. So enter "Select" mode, select the box and on the "Select" sub-menu choose "Back". This moves the box behind its contents, so now the contents appear correctly in a box having the right background colour.

- Select the box you've just drawn and press CTRL-C to make a copy of the box. This will appear on top of the other items and slightly below and to the right of the box you were copying.

- Select the new box and open the "Style" sub-menu again. Set both the line colour and fill colour to the required shadow colour. Black is often used but grey shades also look very attractive. Go into "Select" mode again and move the shadow to the back as you did the box outline previously. It will now be behind the original. While it is selected you can adjust its position if you need to.

If you use several drop shadows on the same page, all should use the same colour and should be offset the same distance and in the same direction from their original boxes.

Pie charts

Pie charts are a most effective way to present numerical information highlighting the proportions of different contributions. An example might be the proportions of sales made by various sales representatives. They are not, however, the easiest form of chart to produce. The technique I use is as follows.

First calculate the angle needed at the centre of each sector by multiplying the percentage represented by 360. Then decide on the size of the circle and the colour of the largest sector. Click on the "ellipse" icon in the toolbox, click "menu", display the "Style" sub- menu and set "Fill colour" to the chosen colour for the largest sector. Line colour is best left at black. Line width is not very important; the default "Thin" is quite adequate.

Turn "Grid Lock" on. Place the pointer where you want the centre of the circle to be and click "select". Pull out your circle to the desired size and click SELECT again.

Leave your largest sector until last. Choose your first sector, click SELECT on the plain "line" icon at the top of the toolbox. Click "menu", display the "Style" sub-menu and change the "Fill colour" to the fill colour you wish to use in this sector. Place the pointer on the circumference of the circle right at the very top, ie at "12 o'clock". Click SELECT to start your line. Move the pointer to the centre of the circle and click SELECT to complete your first sector boundary. Now guess the correct angle clockwise (it does not matter if you are wrong) and place the pointer on or near–but emphatically not outside–the circumference where you guess the other boundary to meet it and click "select". Now click on the auto-close curve icon (fourth from the top in the toolkit) and simply click "adjust". The shape will be closed by a curved line joining the two sector boundaries and protruding somewhat outside the circumference of the circle.

Now this is important. Drag (by holding down "ADJUST") the curve control points on to the circumference, so that the sector you have created does not protrude outside of the circle. We are about to rotate the circle about its centre; if the sector protrudes outside the circumference, the circle will rotate eccentrically causing inaccuracies. Now to get that guessed angle exactly correct! Click on the SELECT icon, click "menu", and display the "Select" sub-menu. From this sub- menu click on "Select all" and then "Group"–this is most important. Turn "Grid Lock" off. Now slide off "Rotate" in the "Select" sub-menu and fill in the number of degrees you calculated earlier for this sector. Rotation is anti-clockwise.

The circle and its solitary sector will be rotated the requisite number of degrees anti-clockwise. Now all you have to do is to adjust the second boundary line until it is vertical. In the "Select" sub-menu click on "Ungroup" and de-select everything except the unfinished sector. On the "Select" sub-menu click on "Edit". Your control points will reappear. Move the pointer on to the point that needs adjustment and drag it until it is on the circumference at 12 o'clock with the boundary exactly vertical. You now have a sector subtending exactly the right number of degrees. There's nothing like doing things properly!

Now to practise using those Bezier curves! You may find it helpful to use the zoom facility to enlarge your view of the curved edge of the sector. Drag the two control points until the temporary lines between the control points and the ends of the curve are exact tangents to the circle (and at exact right angles to the sector boundaries). Your curve may now exactly overlie the circumference of the circle beneath. If so, fine, that's what you want. Click SELECT and your first sector is finished. If not, you will need to lengthen or shorten the control point lines to get the new curve to exactly overlie the circumference. You will soon get the hang of it. When it's just right, click "select". Turn "Grid Lock" back on and repeat this process for all the other sectors except the one in the circle's own fill colours. You need not draw this, just leave it until last and you will find that it has created itself.

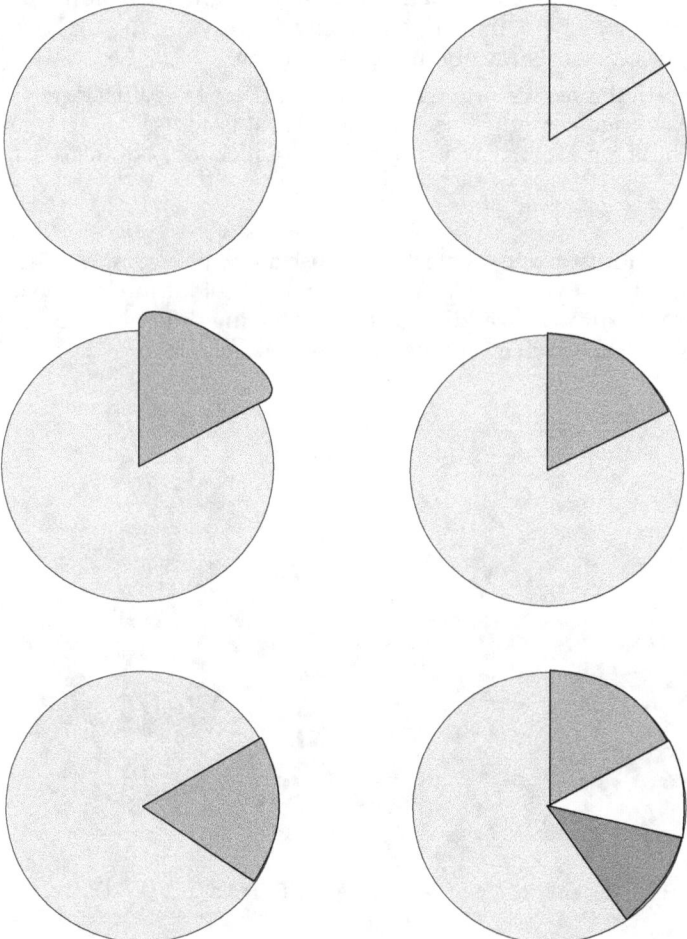

Stages in the creation of a pie chart.
- Create a circle having a suitable fill colour and draw a line from its uppermost point to its centre.

- Draw your next line from the centre to a point near the intersection of the first segment and the circumference.
- Switch to "autoclose curve" and click "adjust" to complete your first segment'".
- Use the Bezier control points to draw the protruding portion of the segment inside the circumference.
- Group the whole figure and rotate it the calculated number of degrees. Get the segment right.
- Repeat the process for the other segments.

Of course, if you're not fussy about exact angles you can omit the rotation stage of the process and just draw your sectors estimating the required angles. Holding a protractor up to the screen may help. But since the software provides the facilities to do the job properly, it seems a shame not make use of them.

If you wish to put labels in the sectors, use white as the text colour against dark coloured sectors and black against lighter sectors–a bold font is advisable. You can add a drop shadow behind a pie chart in the normal way which looks quite effective.

Bar charts

Bar charts are quite straightforward to create. Simply use a row of rectangles side by side. Change the fill colour if you wish or use the same fill colour for each box. You can subdivide boxes vertically by adding rectangles having different colours on top of rectangles. A typical bar chart is shown below.

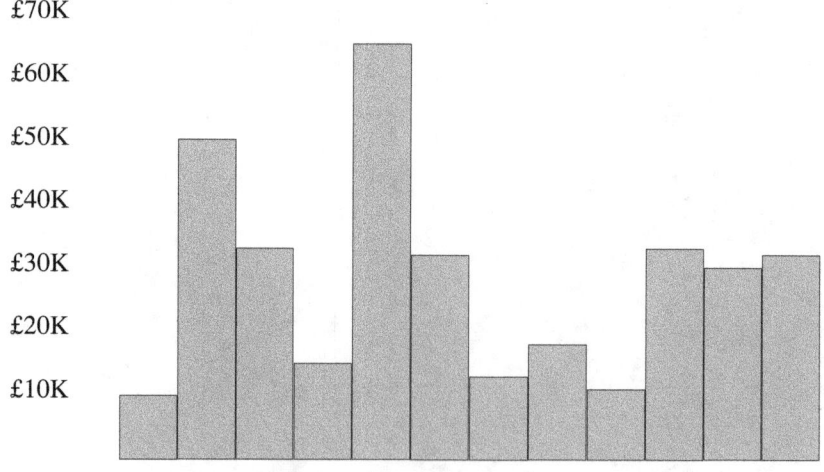

A plain bar chart, however, like that shown above, is rather uninteresting. It can be enhanced by making it "three dimensional". The illustration below shows the same chart with a kind of "drop shadow" except that it follows the line of the chart as though projected backwards a little way. It is created in much the same way as a drop shadow by drawing the outline over the top of the existing chart and then moving it to the back.

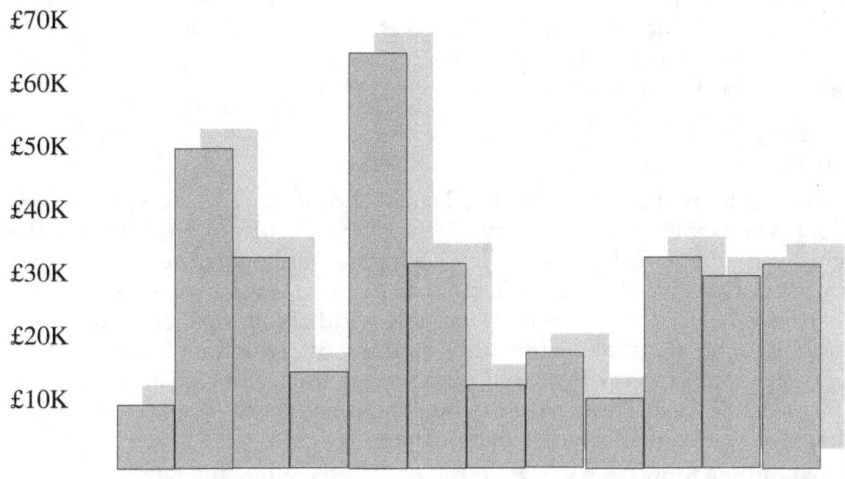

Drop capitals

Drop capitals like that shown below are often used in books and magazine articles to draw the eye to the start of the text. They can be produced in text areas as follows. In the text file omit the first letter (the one that is to be used in enlarged "drop" form) and in the header increase by 1 the number of "columns" in which the text area is to appear.

In the !Draw window introduce your drop capital as a one-character text object. This has the advantage that you can scale it so that it occupies three or four lines as you require. When it is roughly the required size, move it to roughly the right place. Now move your first "column" of text up beside the drop capital. This is, of course/ the portion of text to which the capital belongs. Scale it so that its width fills the gap between the capital and the right-hand edge of the column and its height is equal to or just greater than that of the drop capital. Now bring up the second "column" so that it is immediately beneath the first column and the line spacing is consistent. Scale this so that it occupies the full column width, coming below the drop capital.

Drop capitals were originally used in books and magazine articles to draw the eye to the start of the text. They can be easily produced in !Draw as single character text objects columns of text being wrapped around them.

Paragraph indents

Indented first lines of paragraphs are a legacy of drop capitals. The normal width of indent is one em, but this can vary. There is no difficulty in creating indented paragraphs in unjustified text. Just start each paragraph with a set number of spaces; four often gives the right effect. With justified text, however, this method cannot be used since the spaces have variable width. Nothing looks more untidy than seeing each paragraph begin with a slightly different indent. The solution is to begin each paragraph with a fixed number, say four, NBSP characters, that is, Alt-160 or Alt-SPACE. These have the same nominal width as spaces, but their width is fixed and not affected by justification.

Note that outline fonts from some suppliers do not include the NBSP. You can easily add this yourself if you have the !FontEd application. Load the affected font (both Outlines and IntMetrics files) into the font editor. Expand the font index so that both the normal space (Code 32) and the NBSP (Code 160) "compartments" are on the screen. Move the pointer into Code 32's compartment and, holding down "select", drag the compartment into that of Code 160, then release "select". You have now "copied" the space into the NBSP code. Save both font files.

It is also possible to indent paragraphs using the the \M margin command. At the very beginning of the paragraph to be indented insert a command such as \M12 1/ which indents the line 12 points (1 em). After the first word insert another command such as \M1 1/ which restores default margins with effect from the end of the line.

Hanging indents

These are the opposite of indented paragraphs. The first line of the paragraph is full width and all subsequent lines are slightly indented so that they appear to "hang" from the top line like a flag. The effect is best achieved using the \M margin command in the text area file.

Place a \M margin command near the beginning and end of each paragraph. The one near the beginning sets the required margin for the indented text. \M12 1/, for instance, sets a left margin of 12 points (1 em). This must not come into effect until the end of the line so that it is first applied to the following line. For this reason it should not be placed at the very beginning of the paragraph, but after a few characters have been printed. After the first word is a suitable location.

T-
\-
It
ca-
n-

Drop capitals were originally used in books and magazine articles to draw the eye to the start of the text. They can be easily produced in !Draw as single character text objects columns of text being wrapped around them.

he command at the end of each paragraph is M1 1/ which simply restores default margins. is placed after the full stop and before the rriage return so that it takes effect from the ext line.

This is a test to see if we can create hanging indent paragraphs. What we do is to put a margin command at the beginning and end of each paragraph.

The one at the beginning of the paragraph sets a left margin of, say, 12 points. But it doesn't take effect until the end of the first line. The one at the end of the paragraph restores default values, but doesn't take effect until the next line, which is the start of the next paragraph.

Now as you can see, it works perfectly, but the position of the command at the beginning of each paragraph is critical. If it appears before any characters are printed, the indent will be applied before any characters are printed, so the first line will itself be indented. If it appeals a little later, say after the first word, the first line will be full width and the following lines indented as required.

The one at the beginning of the paragraph sets a left margin of, say, 12 points. But it doesn't take effect until the end of the first line. The one at the end of the paragraph restores default values, but doesn't take effect until the next line, which is the start of the next paragraph.

Now as you can see, it works perfectly, but the position of the command at the beginning of each paragraph is critical. If it appears before any characters are printed, the indent will be applied before any characters are printed, so the first line will itself be indented. If it appeals a little later, say after the first word, the first line will be full width and the following lines indented as required.

Vertical, slanted, inverted and mirror-image printing

One thing that it may seem you simply can't do in !Draw is to print text vertically, upside down, on a slant or in mirror image. In practice nothing's impossible. There are three ways to do this: two "elegant" ways which require additional software and one "hard" way.

Most elegant is a remarkable and surprisingly inexpensive piece of software called IFontFX. This is installed on the icon bar in the same way as other RISC OS applications. It invites you to key in a message of up to 47 characters, choose any of your outline fonts and then apply any combination of a wide range of special effects. These include outlines of various thicknesses, rotation through any angle, wall shadows, floor shadows, slants, lettering in an arc or a circle with or without internal geometrical shapes. All, of course, with a choice of colours from the palette. The list of permutations is endless. The application finally delivers a Drawfile which can be saved to disc or transferred straight into a !Draw window. Once in !Draw the design is regarded as a grouped set of path objects and so it can be scaled to the required size, mirrored/ inverted or rotated as necessary. Each individual character is a separate path object, as is each character's shadow if selected, although all are grouped initially. This means that after ungrouping you can perform further manipulations such as moving the shadow – the possibilities are infinite. !FontFX is excellent value at about £10. *(Now available from APDL and 32 bit compatible).*

VERTICAL TEXT

Outline with Wall Shadow

Ripple with Floor Shadow

Text at any angle

Text·in·a·Circle

Just a selection of striking effects that can be achieved using IFontFX.

Another similar program is TypeStudio, also from APDL. This can create even more exotic exotic effect but is not, at the time of writing, 32 bit compatible.

A third option is DrawWorks. This has a variety of special affects and although some of these are designed to work will "normal" Draw objects they will work equally well with text. The latest version, DrawWorks XL, is also 32 bit compatible.

The "hard" way is that most of these effects can be created in !Draw itself. It's "hard" because it will usually require a lot of work and will usually often you to type in a series of single letters instead of whole words or sentences and then manipulate the letters individually. For example, to create a "ripple" effect you could type in each individual letter of the text and then move them about to produce the required effect.

Reversed and Inverted text

Reversed text is text that is printed in white (or the paper colour) against a black (or the ink colour) background, as shown below.

This is normal text
And this is ▌Inverted Text▐

Inverted text is paper-colour text against an ink-colour background.

In !Draw this effect is easily achieved in text objects, but in text areas it poses difficulties.

If the reversed text is to form a text object, first create the dark area in which the text is to be set. Select the "rectangle" icon from the toolbox, display the "Style" sub-menu and choose black (or whatever you wish) as the "Line colour" and "Fill colour" colours (don't forget to click on "OK"). Now "pull out" your box to approximately the right size in approximately the right place. You can always get its size and position exactly right later. Select "Text", choose from the "Style" sub-menu your "Font name" (remember that bold fonts look better when reversed), "Font size" and your "Font colour", probably white; again don't forget to click on "OK". Place the caret in the dark rectangle and type your text, which will correctly appear white (or light) against the dark background. It will print out correctly too. If the text is too long for the rectangle, you can always expand the rectangle or compress the text.

If the reversed text is part of a text area, you have problems. There are \ commands that allow the text colour and background colour to be changed. If you wish to reverse a short passage of text (white against black) the commands before the passage are:

\C255 255 255/\B0 0 0/

and those after the passage to restore black on white are:

\C0 0 0/\B255 255 255/

On screen the reversed passage will appear to be in "outline": white lettering bounded by a thin black line which is in fact the anti-aliasing.

There will be no solid black background behind the lettering. What you will need to do now is create a black rectangle as described above, move it over the passage concerned and then move it behind the text by clicking "Back" on the "Select" sub-menu. The text will now appear correctly in white against the black background.

9 : Sprites, !Paint and Clip Art

Chapter 5 mentioned that there is an alternative technique for creating graphics, one which involves building up the designs using rectangular arrays of identically sized variously coloured dots called picture elements or pixels. These often, but not always, correspond with the dot structure of the monitor screen. Graphics built up in this manner are known as *bitmaps* or *sprites.*

Sprites may range in size from just a few pixels to a whole screen or even larger. RISC OS computers have a very sophisticated sprite handling capability which allows sprites created in one screen mode to be displayed sensibly in other screen modes. Their original proportions are maintained and their original colours are represented by dither patterns if they are unavailable in the new mode.

The RISC OS application !Paint allows you to create and edit sprites.

Using Sprites in !Draw

Sprites can be freely introduced into !Draw windows and used to illustrate or decorate pages. You simply drag the sprite's icon into the !Draw window. Once in !Draw it can be moved and scaled using the "Select" facility. It can also be mirror-imaged or inverted but not rotated.

There are, however, two factors that you must consider when using sprites in !Draw documents. Firstly, they can use up a considerable amount of memory, especially if they were created in a multi-colour screen mode. Add two or three average size multi-colour sprites to a page of A4 and on a one megabyte machine you may well find yourself running out of memory. If you are creating your own sprites, it helps if you create them in one of the less demanding screen modes. If your sprite needs only two colours, if it is a black and white line drawing for instance, create it in Mode 18 or Mode 0 rather than Mode 20 or Mode 12.

Secondly, printers reproduce sprites rather differently from text and drawings. Sprites are screendumped. This means that each pixel in the sprite (or perhaps each group of pixels if it has been scaled downwards) is converted to a pattern of dots on the paper that represents its colour. The printer, in fact, attempts to create a "screened" version in much the same way that professional printing companies reduce a half tone to a pattern of dots of varying size. This screening process results in half tones that resemble coarse screened newspaper half tones.

Sources of sprites

There are many sources of sprite graphics. You can even use !Paint to grab a screen or part of the screen. This facility is useful as it allows you to import whole screens, or parts of screens, from other software. For example, I once illustrated an article on music using lines of musical notation culled from 'Maestro by saving the screen, loading the resulting file into !Paint, editing out the staves I wanted and saving them for later reloading as sprites into !Draw. The musical symbols, however, looked crude in contrast with the surrounding text. Better looking musical notation can be obtained using path-object musical symbols for this purpose.

Scanners and Video Digitisers

You can convert existing drawings, paintings and even half-tones such as photographs into sprites using a scanner. With a little practice these can give excellent results. If you reproduce an illustration from another publication, however, you could be infringing the originator's copyright. Always obtain permission first.

By means of a video digitiser you can convert TV pictures from videotapes or video discs to sprites. Again, if you plan to reproduce the resulting sprites, be careful about copyright!

Clip Art

Some software distributors offer collections of sprites as "Clip art". These may include half tones, drawings, diagrams, notices or logos. The software distributor supplies them for the express purpose of assisting the user to illustrate or decorate the documents he is producing with the aid of his computer system. Hence the purchase of the clip art of necessity includes the right to reproduce the sprites ad lib on paper without acknowledgement. It does not, however, include the right to distribute the software to a third party unless permission is given first.

Clip art is also available in the form of path objects. The designs are generally simpler than those supplied as sprites, although some are remarkably sophisticated.

Sprite attributes and sprite files

Each sprite is stored as a block of data which contains, besides the colours of the pixels, other vital pieces of information about the sprite. These are called the *sprite attributes*. Each sprite has its own name which follows the conventions for filenames, eg up to 10 letters long. The sprite name will probably have little significance in DTP except as a means of identifying the sprite. Each sprite also carries its width and height (in pixels) and the screen mode in which it was created, since this affects the shape of the pixels used and therefore the proportions of the sprite.

Optionally, a palette may be saved with the sprite. This allows the sprite to use specially created colours and to ensure that, wherever possible, it is subsequently displayed in these colours.

Furthermore, each sprite can optionally have a *mask*, sometimes called a *transparency mask*. This is effectively a map of the sprite showing which pixels are transparent. If a pixel is transparent, the sprite's colour is not displayed. Instead, the colour of the background, or any other object behind the sprite, can be seen. By making pixels around the edge of the sprite transparent, the sprite can be effectively made any required shape. If no mask is present, none of the pixels are transparent and the sprite is by definition a "solid" rectangle.

Each sprite can be saved as an individual sprite file. Several sprites can, however, be collected together and saved in one file.

Using !Paint

The !Paint application is a very versatile piece of software for editing and creating sprites and surprisingly easy to use. In general the User Manual explains !Paint well, but the following may help you on points which are not clear. You are strongly advised when using IPaint, as when using other creative software, to save your work very frequently. A wrong key press can easily ruin your work and it is useful to be able to return quickly to an earlier but recent stage.

Get screen area

!Paint is loaded in the normal manner, its icon appearing on the icon bar. Clicking MENU on the icon offers the usual information about the version in use and the option to leave IPaint with the facility for saving any unsaved work. But it also leads to a very useful utility, "Get screen area". This allows you to save to disc any rectangular portion of the current screen display. To use this, you should first open a directory viewer, or another application window, into which the resulting icon can be dragged. When you click SELECT on this option, the pointer changes to a camera with an arrow. Move this to one corner of the area you wish to save and hold down "select". Keeping select held down, drag the pointer to the opposite corner of the area to be saved–you will drag out a "box" as you do so. When the box encloses the required area release SELECT and the box disappears. A dialogue box now appears in which you can enter a filename. You can save the file by dragging the icon into a directory viewer. The resulting file is a sprite file which can be subsequently loaded into IPaint for further editing if needed. Alternatively, you can automatically add it to an application by dropping it on an appropriate application window, such as a !Draw window. Another option is to drag it onto an icon (such as the !Paint icon itself) to start up a new window containing the sprite.

Editing existing sprites and creating new ones

To load a sprite file into !Paint drag its icon on to the !Paint icon or, with IPaint installed, double-click SELECT on the sprite file icon. This will open a sprite file window in which will be displayed one or more sprite images. These may be full size if the sprite itself is small. However, if the sprite is large, it will be a reduced-size image which may have a distinctly "fuzzy" appearance.

If you wish to start a new sprite file from scratch click SELECT on the !Paint icon and a blank sprite file window will be opened. Use the "Create" sub-menu from the sprite file menu - see below to set up your first sprite.

The Sprite File Menu

Clicking MENU with the pointer in the sprite file window leads to the following menu which is concerned with operations on the file and on any whole sprites it contains rather than the editing of sprites themselves.

- **Info** - This gives information about the sprite file such as its filename (and path), the number of sprites it contains, whether it has been modified since it was loaded and the length of the file in bytes.

- **Save** - This allows the file to be saved using the normal RISC OS conventions.

- **Create** - use this if you wish to create a new sprite from "scratch". A dialogue box will prompt you for a name for the sprite, its width and height in pixels, its screen mode (which need not be the mode currently in use) and whether or not it will have a mask and a palette. These are in fact the standard sprite attributes.

- **Sprite 'name'** - if the pointer was not over a sprite image when you clicked "menu", there will be no sprite name between the quotes and the option will be greyed out showing that it cannot be selected. Otherwise it leads to the following sub-menu of operations that can be performed on the sprite named.

  - **Delete** removes the sprite from the sprite file—it is lost irretrievably unless you have a copy elsewhere.

  - **Copy** prompts you for a new sprite name and creates, in the same file, a copy of the sprite which is identical in all respects except that it has the requested new name. Rename prompts for a new sprite name for the sprite concerned.

  - **Save** allows the sprite to be saved as an individual sprite file.

  - **Info** displays the attributes of the sprite.

  - **Print** leads to a dialogue box which allows a copy of the sprite to be printed, assuming of course that the appropriate printer driver has been installed.

- **Display** - this controls options regarding the contents of the sprite file window. A tick appears by each option currently in force. The default is *Drawing* and *Name*. An alternative is *Full info*. The *Use Desktop Colours* option forces the display of sprites using the current desktop colours and ignoring any palette saved with the sprite. (By default sprites which have palettes are displayed, where possible, using the colours in the sprite's own palette.)

The Sprite Menu

To actually edit a sprite you must double click SELECT over the sprite image in the sprite file window. (The sprite "image" will of course be blank if you have just created a new sprite.) This opens a sprite window containing a full-size image of the sprite concerned. Clicking MENU with the pointer in the sprite window leads to a menu of operations concerning the sprite. Some of these are duplicates of options available from the sprite file window.

- **Info** - displays the attributes of the sprite.

- **Save** - this leads to a sub-menu allowing the sprite and its palette to be saved individually.

- **Paint** - this leads to the "Paint" menu which is concerned primarily with colours. This is considered later.

- **Edit** - this leads to the "Edit" menu which is concerned primarily with the sprite's size and orientation. This is considered later.

- **Zoom** - this leads to a zoom dialogue box exactly like the one in .'Draw. It allows the window to show an enlarged or reduced view of the sprite. For editing work on sprites it is almost essential to use a magnification of at least 4 times.

- **Grid** - this leads to a sub-menu offering a choice of colours for the grid. Note that the grid is only displayed if the zoom facility (above) is set to a magnification of 4 times or more.
- **Print** - this allows the sprite to be printed.

The "Paint" Menu

- **Select ECF** (Extended Colour Fill) – this allows you to use predefined dither patterns as though they were colours from the palette. The pattern must have been previously set up using ! Paint and saved as a sprite. See the User Manual for more detailed information.
- **Select colour** - this allows you to alter the currently selected colour to the colour of the pixel in the sprite which the pointer was pointing to when you clicked MENU. The currently selected colour is the one highlighted (by the presence of its number) in the colour window. You can also use this facility to identify the colour of any pixel about which you may be in doubt.
- **Show colours** - this opens the colour window (if one is not already open). You can alter the currently selected colour by clicking SELECT on the one you want to use.
- **Show tools** - this opens a window showing the very wide range of brushes, pencils, sprayguns and cut and paste facilities available for sprite editing and creation. Note that all this work uses the currently selected colour. A "help" line is provided. This is most useful as it explains the nature of operations which are not always obvious from the icons. See the User Manual for more detailed information.
- **Small colours** - this controls the size of the colour window. It is most useful when working in 256 colour modes since these obviously demand a very large colour window.
- **Edit palette** - this leads to the familiar palette dialogue box in which colours can be redefined.

The "Edit" Menu

- **Flip vertically** - this produces a reflection of the sprite.
- **Flip horizontally** - this produces a mirror image of the sprite.
- **Rotate** - this leads to a writable sub-menu in which you enter the number of degrees anti-clockwise through which you wish to rotate the sprite. The default is 90 degrees. For clockwise rotation either enter a negative number, eg -90, or subtract the angle from 360. Note that rotation is a very time consuming operation!
- **Adjust size** - this changes the boundary box of the sprite. Be careful! Making the sprite smaller may cause detail to be lost from around the edges. Once it has been lost, it cannot be regained (unless you have it saved on disc). Two methods are provided – you can either click on directional arrows or write the new size in pixels. Note that despite the positioning of the arrows, all vertical adjustments are made to the top edge of the sprite and all horizontal adjustments to its right-hand edge.

- **Insert columns/Insert rows** - these allow additional rows and columns of pixels to be inserted at any position in the sprite. Note that the new columns or rows will be inserted at the position of the pointer when you clicked "menu". A vertical or horizontal line will appear through the sprite at the position where the new material is to be inserted. A dialogue box will ask for the number of columns or rows to insert. You can either type a number and then press <RETURN> or move the pointer within the sprite file window to indicate the number and then click "select".

- **Delete columns/Delete rows** - these allow adjacent columns or rows to be deleted from the sprite. The operation is most useful for trimming the edges from very large sprites such as those created by scanner-driver software. When you use the former method the lines deleted will automatically be taken from above or to the right of the line. Using the latter, a second line will follow the pointer indicating the limit of the area to be deleted. Note that this operation is somewhat temperamental. You must take the pointer straight off the menu and into the sprite window without touching any other part of the menu structure. Otherwise the operation is cancelled. A dialogue box shows the number of columns or rows. You can either edit this number and then press RETURN or move the pointer within the sprite file window until the required number is indicated and then click SELECT. Note that the columns or rows will be deleted starting from the position of the pointer when you clicked "menu". A vertical or horizontal line will appear through the sprite at this position.

- **Mask** - this toggles the mask on and off.

- **Palette** - this toggles the palette on and off.

10: Understanding Printers

One major difference– perhaps even the major difference– between wordprocessing and DTP lies in the way the printer is used. In wordprocessing the printer generally reproduces pure text using its own built-in typefaces. In DTP those built-in typefaces are normally not used. Instead the printer reproduces the page whose image has been composed on screen, using typefaces contained in the computer software. The printer operates in a graphics mode, building up the document dot-by-dot from graphics data which the computer has generated. Besides text the printer may find itself handling rules, boxes, tints, line drawings and possibly even half-tone illustrations.

The quality of reproduction will depend largely on the type and condition of the printer used and also on the graphics resolution. This book is concerned with low-cost DTP and in a budget system the printer is most likely to be a 9-pin dot matrix type such as the Epson FX-80 or one of many compatible types. Although the Epson FX-80 itself is long obsolete, its specification has become an "industry standard".

9-pin Dot Matrix Printers

The FX-80's print head contains nine wires or pins arranged vertically one point (1/72 inch) apart. Normally these are withdrawn inside the head. Each pin is controlled by a solenoid and when its solenoid is energised under software control, the pin is forced outwards so that it strikes the paper through the inked ribbon, printing a dot. The actual size and shape of each dot depends on a miscellany of widely variable factors such as the condition of the ribbon and the type of paper in use. Even with a fresh ribbon, however, there is space clearly visible between adjacent vertical dots, showing the dots to be less than one point in diameter.

When printing graphics, normally only eight of the nine wires are used. Since in software one byte contains eight bits, it is convenient to let each bit in a byte control one wire. The convention is that the most significant bit (value 128) controls the top wire and the least significant bit (value 1) controls the bottom wire. Each byte can be regarded as representing a number between 0 and 255 and this allows any of the 256 possible combinations of the wires in the printer head to be fired simultaneously.

Horizontal dot resolution is variable. It is regulated very simply by the speed at which the print head travels past the paper. The more slowly the head travels, the closer adjacent dots will be. In practice the FX-80 offers a choice of 60 (single density), 72 (plotter), 80 and 90 (CRT graphics, that is, screendumps), 120 (double density) and 240 (quadruple density) dots per inch and some variants offer other densities. The FX-85, for instance, offers 144 dots per inch (double- density plotter).

It may seem at first thought that vertical resolution must inevitably be limited to the spacing of the wires, ie 72 dots per inch. Indeed a vertical graphics resolution of 72 dots per inch is offered. This gives rapid printing, but the quality is poor, resembling the printer's draft text mode.

In practice, superior vertical resolution is made possible by mechanical "trickery". The printer roller is capable of advancing the paper in increments of 1/2l6 inch. So if after one pass of the print head the paper is advanced by 1/2l6 inch (1/3 point), the print head may now make a second pass printing new rows of dots between those printed in the first pass. This creates an effective vertical graphics resolution of 144 dots per inch, similar to that of the "near letter quality" text mode offered by some printers.

Even finer resolution can be achieved by advancing the paper a further V216 inch and printing a third set of dots in the gap remaining between the first two sets. Clearly the computer software has to divide the image up so that dots are printed in their appropriate passes.

The vertical resolution of 216 dots per inch made possible by this technique is a useful complement to the 240 dots per inch horizontal resolution. In the resulting 240 x 216 dots per inch graphics capability, adjacent dots overlap vertically, allowing the printing of black areas that appear convincingly solid. A refreshing change from the grizzled graphics often seen coming from dot matrix machines being used in a more conventional manner. In fact a 9-pin dot-matrix printer at 240 x 216 dots per inch is capable of giving quite impressive results.

But there are three disadvantages. One is that high-density graphics wears out ribbons very rapidly. The second is that printing is slow, three passes of the print head being needed for each 1/9th of inch of paper printed. The third is that, despite all that has been said already, the printer cannot in fact print adjacent dots in the same row. While the printer can in theory print a single dot at any of the 1920 positions across an 8 inch page, it cannot print two adjacent dots. This is because the tiny distance, 1/240 inch, between adjacent dot positions is covered so quickly that by the time the wire has been withdrawn and is ready to fire again the head has passed the next position. So the printer itself filters out any dot that follows immediately after a printed dot. Consequently when printing solid graphics shapes (and this includes text in a DTP system) the first dot is printed and then alternate dots are printed until the final boundary of the shape has been passed.

Now this has unfortunate repercussions. In the "portrait" printing of intricate shapes it means that irregularities in the left-hand edge of the shape may produce noticeable "echoes" at the right hand edge. This is particularly noticeable in the letter "y" in some sizes. Opposite the point where the left-hand stroke meets the right-hand stroke a slight indentation is visible, marring what should be a perfectly straight trailing edge to the character. Oddly in "landscape" printing the effect is far less noticeable. It is still present, but characters are now printed from bottom to top, forcing the distortion into the top of the character where it is less obvious.

When graphics from a dot matrix printer are examined closely, however, the print will always appear somewhat "dotty". This is because the dots themselves are not perfect filled circles nor are they consistent in size. Moreover rules and boxes are likely to reveal the awful truth that the print head drive mechanism is never perfectly accurate. The condition of the ribbon will affect the depth of colour of the printout, sometimes variations are quite noticeable within the course of a single page. Remember that dot matrix printers were designed primarily as text printers, not as advanced graphics tools!

There is a way, however, in which the inaccuracies and "dotty" appearance can sometimes be overcome. If your publication uses A5 page size, design and print out the pages at A4 size and then reduce the printout on a photocopier. The precise ratio of the A4 to A5 reduction facility offered on many photocopiers is 1.414:1, which for practical purposes can be regarded as 1.4:1. So if you want 10 point text in the final A5 copy, you will need to set the original at 14 point. The reduction process greatly reduces the "dottiness" in text and makes irregularities in rules and boxes far less apparent. At the time of writing I am still using letterheads that were prepared in !Draw as an A4 landscape design, printed on an Epson FX-800 and reduced in this way for use as A4 portrait. The effective final graphics resolution is 339 x 305 dots per inch, theoretically better than a laser printer at 300 dots per inch, although in practice the output from a laser printer is markedly superior in appearance.

24-pin Dot Matrix Printers

24-pin dot matrix printers are an alternative to and an improvement on the 9-pin types. They work in precisely the same way, but the print head incorporates 24 tiny pins generally arranged in two vertical rows of 12, slightly offset. The separation between adjacent pins is 1/90 inch and the offset is 1/180 inch so in a single pass, a 24-pin machine can achieve a vertical graphics resolution of 180 dots per inch. This is only marginally inferior to the 216 dots per inch achieved by a 9-pin machine in three passes.

Some 24-pin printers, such as LQ500-compatible types, are limited to this vertical resolution. Others, however, such as the LQ850- compatible types can advance the paper 1/360 inch and make a second pass of the print head. This results in a startling graphics resolution of 360 dots per inch, surpassing the resolution of many laser printers. 24-pin machines are a little more expensive than 9-pin types, but then for textual work they are capable of far higher quality, some offering a very wide range of built-in typefaces. Not surprisingly, the graphics produced by 24-pin machines is also significantly superior to that of 9- pin types. Unfortunately they are still subject to some of the shortcomings of the dot matrix principle such as inaccuracies in drive speed and uneven inking of the ribbon. In general the quality obtained from a laser or ink jet printer at 300 dots per inch is superior to that of a 24-pin dot matrix machine at 360 dots per inch.

Ink jet printers

Ink jet printers provide a level of sophistication and a price range intermediate between 24-pin dot matrix printers and laser printers. One of the best known is the Hewlett Packard DeskJet Plus. This is effectively a 28-pin dot matrix machine, the vertical separation between the dots being just $1/150$ inch. In its high-quality text and graphics modes it prints with two passes of the print head, advancing the paper $1/300$ inch between passes to give a 300 x 300 dots per inch graphics resolution.

The machine prints, as its name suggests, by squirting tiny jets of ink at the paper to form the dots. The minute, accurately formed dots and consistent inking result in a printout that is hardly distinguishable from that of a laser printer, it being often impossible to see the dot structure at all. The machine, in fact, emulates a LaserJet and is controlled from RISC OS using the appropriate LJ printer driver. For DTP work, if you can afford this type of machine, it is worth considering. Another virtue compared with dot matrix printers is that it is far quieter in operation.

Since the ink is emphatically in the liquid state when it hits the paper, the quality of the paper used in ink-jet printers is highly critical. Some paper, although it gives acceptable results with dot-matrix printers, acts as blotting paper to an ink-jet printer. Both text and graphics appear blurred and unsightly and you may also find unwanted "whiskers" protruding from solidly inked areas. If you use an ink-jet printer, shop around and try paper from different suppliers to see which gives the best results. This is especially important if you plan to reproduce the artwork which your printer is producing.

Laser printers

Laser printers are the most sophisticated, and the most expensive computer printers available. Because of their expense they are really out of place in a book on budget DTP. However, the development of DTP is inextricably bound up with the development of the laser printer. In addition, it is not necessary to actually own one in order to make use of it (see later). Therefore, they are worthy of a mention.

The process by which a laser printer puts marks on paper is an electrostatic one very similar to that of a photocopier. The image is built up on an electrostatically charged drum by a laser beam (in fact the light source is not always a laser) scanning through either the images of the printer's built-in typefaces or images built up in "screen memory" or a mixture of both.

In terms of speed, accuracy and quality of printout laser printers are unsurpassed. But if you should decide to purchase one, there are two points that you need to consider.

The way laser printers work demands that all the data for the whole page be sent before the machine can begin to print. Most laser printers offer graphics at 300 x 300 dots per inch, although the latest machines are offering higher resolution graphics such as 600 x 600 dots per inch. The data for an A4 page at 300 x 300 dots per inch resolution requires one megabyte of memory.

Another unfortunate fact is that, although the printing is fast, the building of the image is not. To calculate, transmit and build up the image for a well-filled page of A4 may take a couple of minutes during which time both computer and printer are busy. If something horrendous has gone wrong with your page design, you will have to wait for this lengthy process to be completed before you see the printout and discover that all is not as it should be. With other printer types you see the printout begin to emerge soon after you give the instruction to print. If you see something amiss, you can quickly abort the operation (take the printer off line and then press Escape), make the necessary adjustments and start again.

There are two principal "families" of laser printer: those using the PostScript page description language devised by Adobe and those using the Hewlett Packard LaserJet conventions. RISC OS caters for both.

As with other printer types, prices are continually falling. Consequently laser printers are becoming ever more affordable. One development which may be of interest to readers of this book is the "Direct Drive" laser printer system, probably the best known example being the Laser Direct range from Computer Concepts. These systems all use a comparatively low-cost laser printer such as the Canon LBP- 4 which has only 256 Kilobytes of memory. Only the mechanical components of the printer (the "engine") are used, however, most of its electronics being disabled. The printer engine is controlled by a "podule" (an interface board) which must first be installed in the computer. ROM-based software in the podule uses the computer's memory to store the image of the page being printed using a special compressed data format. The result is very fast printing of whole graphic pages on a low-cost laser printer. There is even a 600 x 600 dots per inch version (Laser Direct Hi-Res) which by careful shopping can be obtained for around £1000 (plus VAT). If you wonder what the catch is, it's this – your computer must have at least 2 Megabytes of RAM to allow room for your applications and the printer image of the documents.

Printer drivers

One of the differences between RISC OS and some other operating systems (such as that in the BBC Microcomputer) is the need to load specific printer driver software in order to print out documents being created in applications. Various printer drivers are supplied with RISC OS and others, for machines not covered by the four, are available from software suppliers.

They are loaded in the same way as other RISC OS applications, but when installed their icons appear at the left-hand side of the icon bar, to the right of the disc drive icons.

When you have selected the option appropriate for your printer you can "save" it using the "Save choices" option from the icon menu (click MENU on the printer driver icon). Once saved, the preferred option will automatically be selected whenever you install the printer driver.

The drivers can be used in two ways. To print a pure text file such as one created in !Edit, simply drag the file icon on to the printer driver icon. It is not necessary for the text to exist as an actual disc file. A whole document or a selected part of a document can be printed by making as if to save it, but then dragging the icon on to the printer driver rather than into a directory viewer. (In fact the text file is saved to disc temporarily.)

For printing graphics produced in applications such as !Draw or !Paint the printer driver must be accessed from within the application by calling up the appropriate menu option. In !Draw "Print" is the last item in the "Misc" menu. If no printer driver is installed a warning message is issued.

Oddly enough, for printing graphics, the printer driver icon need not be present on the icon bar. Provided it has been displayed, the application will be able to print graphics. This is because the printer driver itself is a "module" which remains installed after the icon has been deleted from the icon bar. The icon and its associated software is only needed again if you wish to change the selected graphics mode.

How the printer driver works

The printing of graphics pages created in !Draw is in fact a highly complex process. The following relates to the dot matrix and Laser Jet printer drivers, not necessarily the PostScript driver.

The computer sends the printer "strips" of bitmap graphics at the resolution selected by the printer driver. This resolution will probably exceed that of the screen display and is quite independent of the screen mode. Each strip could be regarded as a portion of "virtual screen" having the same resolution as the printer. In creating each graphics "strip" the computer must examine every object on the page in turn to see if its bounding box overlaps the strip being considered. If it does, then the lines in drawings and characters are re-plotted on the "virtual screen". Colours and grey tones are represented as "dither patterns", that is patterns of alternating black and white dots which give the appearance of an intermediate grey tone. Sprites are screendumped, each pixel in the sprite being represented by a group of bits that make up a dot in the "virtual screen" (the dot size is related to the pixel colour, darker colours being represented by bigger dots). If, however, the bounding boxes of all objects are outside the current strip, the printer advances the paper until either it encounters an object or it reaches the end of the sheet.

Clearly, the higher the resolution of the printer, the greater the number of calculations that the computer must perform and the amount of data that must be sent to the printer. Thus the time taken is longer. A simple calculation shows that an area of 11 x 8 inches covered with dots at 300 dots per inch contains 7,920,000 dots! So when you print a page of well utilised A4 at 300 dpi, you are sending very nearly one megabyte of data to the printer.

Time taken in printing is proportional to the square of the resolution and is not particularly dependent on the printer type. It is the computer itself that limits the process. I recently printed the same page of A4 (portrait) using a DeskJet Plus first at 300 dpi and then at 150 dpi. The times taken were approximately 17 and 4 minutes respectively.

Printing can be accelerated by making plenty of memory available to the computer on a machine with limited RAM. This allows it to plot several adjacent graphics strips together and reduces the number of occasions on which each object must be examined.

Printing takes appreciably longer if your page layout is "landscape" (horizontal) rather than "portrait" (vertical). If your printer is limited to A4 sheets, it will always print across the page whether its design is portrait or landscape. The printing process itself is identical, the computer scanning through each object in turn as it builds up the graphics strips to send to the printer. But in a landscape design, each strip runs vertically up the page and consequently is likely to be affected by many more objects. For example, it may pass through footlines, text, diagrams and many types of heading. Hence it may involve a dozen or more fonts. Moreover, the outline font manager is optimised for "portrait" printing. Each text character must be rotated 90 degrees for landscape printing and this takes appreciable time.

Using a "Distant Printer"

One of the options available from the printer driver icon menus is to send the printer data to a file instead of a printer. This can be useful. If you are creating a high-quality document and have only a low resolution printer. You can produce "proof" copies locally, then, when approved for press, you can load, say, a laser printer driver and save the data to a file on a floppy disc. This can now be sent to a laser printer owner for the final printout.

Transferring files to MS DOS discs for processing on PC compatible machines using the MS DOS "PRINT" command does not work well– some bytes are intercepted by MS DOS leading to distortion of the image. Moreover, the MS DOS disc format supported by the PC emulator and utilities such as !PCDir is limited to 720 Kilobytes per disc.

An exception is the PostScript printer driver. This will convert !Draw documents to PostScript files which are typically a manageable 40 to 50 kilobytes long per page of A4. Clearly several such pages can be accommodated on one Archimedes or MS DOS disc. PostScript files consist of ASCII text and transfer to MS DOS without difficulty. I have frequently used this means of reproducing pages with very high quality.

11: Reproducing Your Work

The fact that you are interested in DTP (and presumably you are since you are reading this book!) indicates that you are involved in some way in the world of publishing. Of course it may be that you delight in preparing text and devising page layouts simply to satisfy some innate whim. However, it is far more likely that you are interested in using your computer system for some genuine publishing purpose such as the production of newsletters or magazines for your club, school or church or letterheads, forms or promotional literature for your business.

If so, you will almost certainly want many copies of the wonderful artwork that comes oh-so slowly out of your printer. Let us consider how to do this. After all, the verb publish literally means "make public", the ideal being to let everyone have a copy who would like one.

There are three main methods of producing multiple copies: using your computer printer, using a photocopier and using offset litho printing. The method you choose depends partly on the quality you want and the urgency with which you want it. But by far the most significant factor is the number of copies you require.

How many copies?

If you want only one copy then you need look no further than your existing computer printer. The single copy that it produces will suffice, and if you want more than one, but only, say, two or three copies of a document that is no more than four or five pages long, then you may be content to wait a while for your computer system to churn them out individually.

Photocopiers

For quantities of up to about 500 copies, the most economic method of reproduction is to use a photocopier. If you run a business you may already have one. If you are in employment, your employer may grant you access to one at a modest cost, especially if the job is charity related. Failing that, every High Street nowadays has one or more "instant print shops" offering photocopying facilities at a competitive price.

There are several distinct sorts of photocopier, but the system that has now all but replaced its rivals is known technically as xerography. A drum is given a positive electrostatic charge. A lens projects on to the surface of the drum an image of the document being copied. Where light falls on the drum, ie in the white parts of the image, the light destroys the electrostatic charge. But in the dark parts of the image, the charge remains. The drum is then dusted with powdered ink called toner which bears a negative charge. Since opposite charges attract, the toner collects on those areas of the drum which are positively charged, and which correspond to the black areas of the image. The drum now contacts the paper, transferring the toner image to it. The paper, which is ordinary plain paper, is heated. This melts the toner which now becomes firmly stuck to the paper and goes hard on cooling.

The drum is the heart of the xerographic process. In early machines it was a frequent cause of problems in photocopying since any blemish on its delicate surface was likely to leave a mark on each copy made. In many modern machines, however, the drum is itself a part of the toner cartridge and is discarded and replaced when the toner cartridge is changed.

Nowadays, the quality of reproduction is generally excellent. It is far superior to that obtainable as recently as five years ago. Even half-tone illustrations can, with care, be reproduced quite acceptably. Photocopiers vary widely in the facilities they offer. The most sophisticated office machines can handle sheets up to A3 size copying on to both sides simultaneously at speeds of up to one copy per second. Some automatically collate and even staple multi-page documents. Many offer a choice of colour of reproduction by means of interchangeable toner cartridges. Most offer "zoom" facilities allowing enlarged or reduced size copies. This type of machine is favoured by the instant print shops since it is ideal for short-run work, the kind of work in which a DTP user is most likely to be interested. At the opposite end of the price scale are small personal copiers. The simplest generally take only A4 paper and offer no "zoom" facilities.

You may be able to set the machine to produce up to 9 or perhaps 99 copies. Some of these use interchangeable toner cartridges giving a choice of colours. For producing small numbers of single-sided, single- colour copies, such a machine would be perfectly adequate. A run of 250 double-sided copies on such a machine would, however, be distinctly tedious.

Between these two extremes are many machines offering intermediate levels of sophistication. The Canon PC-7 which I use is a very compact machine which, remarkably in a machine at its price, features automatic exposure control (which can be over-ridden) and zoom from 70 to 122 per cent in steps of 1 per cent. Runs of up to 99 copies can be pre-set, although the auto-feed mechanism is not reliable– many long runs being terminated with a jammed sheet before completion! Toner cartridges are available in four colours besides black and the quality of reproduction is impeccable. Mine is used mainly for single copies and runs of 20 to 50 copies.

The quality of photocopying is affected by the type of paper used. The familiar rule "you gets what you pays for" applies here as in most other areas of life. Inferior paper gives inferior results. You cannot expect fine detail, for instance, on paper having a coarse texture. On a photocopier with automatic feed the handling characteristics of the paper become important. My personal attempt to conserve planet Earth's limited resources by using what claimed to be 100 per cent recycled photocopier paper proved catastrophic. Despite the worthiness of the cause I was compelled to resort, reluctantly, to "new" material. Don't be afraid to shop around and try different makes. You may find that a different brand gives a dramatic improvement at little or no extra cost.

In buying a photocopier or even finding a suitable machine in a print shop watch out for one problem. Machines fitted with zoom sometimes cause distortion, the vertical lines tending to slew clockwise. This is particularly noticeable if you photocopy a photocopy since the effect is cumulative, each generation slewing the verticals further. The test is to photocopy a piece of graph paper and then photocopy the copy. Superimpose the second-generation copy and the original and hold them up to the light to see if they correspond.

Offset litho printing

For runs of 500 or more copies you may find that it is cheaper to use offset litho printing. Unless you work in a printing shop, you are unlikely to have access to such a machine and so you will have to use a commercial printing company.

Offset litho is now the most widely used printing technique. The page being printed is copied on to a flexible metal (or sometimes paper) "plate" by a process similar to photocopying. In fact ordinary photocopiers arc sometimes used for this purpose. The image on the plate is still the "right way round". The plate is then fixed to a drum, commonly called the "cylinder", which contact" a rubber "blanket" roller which in turn contacts the paper

Lithography uses the principle that oil and water do not mix. The ink is oil based and therefore immiscible with water Ink and water are separately applied to the entire surface of the plate cylinder before it contacts the blanket roller. On the surface of the plate, however, the ink is attracted to those areas where the plate is dark and water is attracted to those where it is light. A temporary mirror image in ink and water is formed on the blanket roller. When this mirror image transfers itself to the paper, it creates a right-way-round image on it. One of the advantages of offset lithography is that its rotary action lends itself to high-speed work. On earlier letterpress machines it was necessary to insert the paper, "stamp" the image on to it, then remove the paper. This was a reciprocating start-.stop-start process. In offset litho the paper, either as separate sheets or as a continuous roll called the "web", keeps moving like a never-ending stream of clothes through a mangle,

The cost of litho printing will include elements towards the cost of the paper and ink and also of the plates. Since the cost of the plate and its processing i? the same no matter how many copies are made from it, the unit cost per copy will fall as the print run gets longer.

Preparing work for photocopying or printing

The preparation of work for reproduction, whether by photocopier or litho, is essentially the same. Both processes start, so far as we are concerned, with the "fair copy" which your DTP system has produced.

Photocopiers and litho printers are effectively "digital" machines in that they see matters in terms of black (or whatever the toner or ink colour) and white (or whatever the paper colour). They cannot reproduce intermediate shades. This has two important repercussions for DTP users, both of which can be summarised as "your sins will find you out!".

Firstly, if you use a dot matrix printer with a well worn ribbon you cannot expect good results. For instance, if you attempt to print a solid black area on a dot matrix printer with a worn out ribbon the result will be a mass of tiny black dots separated by diminutive but nevertheless real areas of uninked paper. It may appear like a grey mass to you and you may be tempted to think that by turning the photocopier (or platemaker) exposure control to "dark" you will get solid black copies. You won't. The copies will look no better than the original and probably considerably worse. If you are doing an important DTP job that must look good, the golden rule is fit a new ribbon first! If you are one of the many computer users who insist on using printer ribbons down to the last molecule of ink, then keep the old one in a safe place and put it back in the printer after you've printed out the DTP job.

Secondly, half tones (such as photographs) should normally be screened. This is the process which converts areas of solid grey or colours to patterns of tiny black dots on a white background which the photocopier or litho equipment can reproduce satisfactorily. Screening demands access to professional printing equipment. Your friendly neighbourhood print shop will certainly do it for you if he is also doing the printing. He may be willing to do it if you are going to do the reproduction work yourself on a photocopier. Work out the space that each item being screened will occupy and in your layout draw a rectangle of the appropriate size in the right place. Print inside it a clear label such as "Figure 3 here" or "Photo of Chairman here" for identification purposes. Also, whenever you send photographs to a printer, make sure that they are correctly and clearly labelled on the reverse. If there are several photos of personalities, remember that although you personally know which is Joe Bloggs and which is Fred Nurk, the printer may not. Even clearly identified photographs sometimes get interchanged by printers.

You may get away without screening if:

- the picture has already been screened, eg if it was cut out of a newspaper and pasted in place (in which case you may technically be guilty of breach of copyright if you reproduce it without permission)
- the picture contains abundant tiny detail (in which case it has effectively screened itself)
- the picture was reproduced on a high-resolution (300 dots per inch or better) printer out of !Draw or !Paint in which case the software itself provides a somewhat coarse level of screening.

Try to avoid cutting and pasting of the literal variety. In both photocopying and litho work the edges of pasted pieces often become visible as faint lines which are unsightly. One of the great benefits of DTP is that the software equivalent of cutting and pasting leaves no such marks!

For very high quality work, where the output of even a laser printer would not be adequate, there is a further option available to you. This is to send the page data to a printing company for setting on a linotron or other high-definition typesetting machine. Many of these operate at about 1200 dots per inch and most require their input as PostScript files. A PostScript driver is supplied with RISC OS. From its icon menu select the option of sending its output to a file on disc rather than to a PostScript printer.

Full Colour work

!Draw provides by default black, white, six intermediate shades of grey and eight colours which you can use on the screen to make up beautifully coloured pages of text, drawings and sprites. But, unless you have a colour printer, when you print out coloured matter your printer will print only in monochrome, using dither patterns to represent coloured or grey matter. And watch out for bugs which cause black text to become "dithered" adjacent to non-black text.

If you have a colour printer you may be able to print in several colours, producing a tolerably accurate full-colour representation of the screen display. Reproducing these coloured printouts is, however, a complex matter. If you require only very few copies, it is best to simply let your colour printer chum them out. If you require more and if it is imperative that the copies faithfully reproduce the colour original that came off your printer, you can use colour photocopying.

The alternative is colour litho. You will be charged about £75 for "colour separation", that is separation of your artwork into its red, yellow, blue and black components. You will also be charged for four plates, one for each colour. The print run will require four lots of ink and careful alignment (the technical term is "registration") to ensure that the separate colours are accurately superimposed. So expect a hefty bill! Some small printers, incidentally, do not themselves handle four-colour work, they subcontract it to a larger printer. This will further add to the bill as both printers will, not unreasonably, aim to make a profit from the job.

Spot colour

If you want to add colour to your work in a more cost-effective manner, you can use what the printing trade calls *spot colour*. This is the use of a limited amount of a second colour (or even second and third colours) on an otherwise black-and-white page.

Design your page as though it were monochrome. When you have completed your layout work, but before you have printed it out, save it to disc in the normal way. Now examine it on screen to see if there is a heading or a piece of graphics that would look good in a different colour. Another possibility is a coloured tint behind a drawing. Use the colours sparingly. More than two or three items in colour on an otherwise black-and-white page can look untidy.

Now, if you are adding a coloured item (such as a block of tint) to the page, add it as though it were in black, and save the page again under its normal filename.

If you are changing items from black to colour, delete them from the page. The screen should now show only those items which you want printed in black. Print it out and save it to disc under a different filename.

Next, reload the original and delete everything that is to be printed in black so that only the coloured item(s) remain in their original places. Print it out (in black!) and save it to disc under, yet another, different filename.

You now have two printouts, one of the black matter and one of the coloured matter. And you have the page saved in three different files, one "complete" one, one showing only the black matter and one showing only the coloured matter.

If you are going to photocopy the material, photocopy the black matter first in the normal way. Next, change your toner cartridge to the required "second colour". Then photocopy the coloured matter, passing the black copies back through the machine so that the coloured matter is superimposed on the black. With a photocopier, it is impossible to get registration accuracy better than about 1 millimetre. This means that adding second colours to graphs or diagrams is not really practical. But for headings or coloured boxes around black headings, registration errors up to 1 mm are unlikely to be noticed.

For litho printing you will need to present your printer with the two sets of artwork, one representing black matter and one representing colour. It will normally be obvious which is which, but you will need to agree with the printer which second colour you wish him to use. You can expect significantly better registration than in photocopying so that use of second colours in graphics is feasible. You will be charged extra for the second colour, of course, since a second plate will be needed and the printer will need to make a second print run if he does not have a two-colour press. It will cost extra, but not nearly so much as four-colour work.

It may appear that there is another, simpler, way in which your computer can produce "colour separations". If you compose your page knowing from the start which items will use spot colour, let us say all headings will be in red, you can select red on the screen for your headings, leaving all the black matter in black as normal. Then, using the colour-change facilities on the palette, redefine the red headings to white and do a printout of the remaining black material. Restore default colours and then redefine black to white and red to black. A printout now will consist of the red matter printed as black. Let me assure you that this process does not work. The two printouts will be identical, the black matter appearing in normal black and the red in a dither pattern representing red. This is because the palette only affects the screen display. For printing, the screen display is ignored and the colour data is derived from that in force when the objects were created.

12: Trouble Shooting

There are many problems that can arise; this section deals with just a few of them.

Problems in !Edit and in Text File Transfer to !Draw

!Edit crashes on startup

If you're "into DTP" you may well end up by becoming a "font collector". Fonts are only recognised by the outline font manager if they are stored in the application directory !Fonts.

!Edit checks the contents of IFonts when it starts up. If the number of fonts, including the System Font, is too large !Edit crashes with the error message: "Edit has suffered a fatal internal error (type=5) and must exit immediately".

The solution is to store all your fonts in an innocuously named directory such as "Fontstore" and to store the ones you use most often in !Fonts. If you need an unusual font for a certain job, temporarily transfer it into !Fonts before starting up !Draw.

Of course, a more elegant solution, afont management software such as FontFS or EasyFont Pro from APDL.

Text file won't load into !Draw.

!Draw. will only accept plain text files. These can be produced by !Edit or any other text editor.

The text file must also terminate with a carriage return.

Bad font number error

Sooner or later you will get the dreaded "Bad Font Number" error message as you attempt to load a text file into !Draw. When this happens the transfer of the text file is aborted. Sometimes the cause can be very difficult to find. The error can arise even though there are no font changes in the text. The error message is misleading–"Bad font number or unrecognised command" would be more appropriate.

One common cause is a bad new line. To force a new line in your text area, you must end the previous line with "\<CR>", since !Draw interprets a <CR> on its own as a space. Sometimes a space may be introduced between the "\" and the <CR>. This is especially likely if you have inserted the new line into the middle of an old one. You probably inserted the <CR> before the first character of the new line, then you remembered that you needed a "\" at the end of the previous line, so you placed the caret immediately after the last visible character in the line forgetting that a space, invisible on the screen, follows it. So in the text file !Draw encounters the sequence "\<space><CR>" instead of "\<CR>" and regards the <space> as a bad font number. Eliminate this problem by searching your document for "\" at the end of a line. When found, place the caret on that line and press Ctrl-[right] to move the caret to the end of the line. If it stops immediately to the right of the "\", keep searching. If it stops one or more spaces to the right of the "\" you have located a problem so delete the space(s).

Another possible cause of the "Bad Font Number" error is a simple typing error. You can change fonts whenever you wish, provided you define your font numbers correctly. If you define font 0 as Trinity Medium and font 1 as Trinity Medium Italic you can put the single word "Typeface" in italics in a roman environment thus:

\ITypeface\0

But if you typed very quickly and carelessly interchanged the "\" and the "T" thus: \Tlypeface\0, !Draw will interpret the \T as a bad font number.

Another cause is in the header. Remember that in "\" commands characters are case sensitive. If you ignore this and include in the header the line:

\F0 Trinity Medium 12

the "f" will be regarded as a bad font number.

Wrong font used in text area object

Sometimes font changes are ignored. This may happen if a number follows immediately after a font change command. Thus to change to font 1 and print "1990" your text might read "M1990". But this is ambiguous–!Draw does not know whether this is font 1 followed by "1990" or font 11 followed by "990". The "fix" is to terminate the font change command with a "/": \1/1990.

Unable to load font

Sometimes when transferring a text area file into !Draw you may get the error message "Unable to load the font <font name>". Unlike the bad font number error, this does not prevent the transfer of the file. The text area is still created, but sections of it that were supposed to be in the font that could not be loaded will be reproduced in another font, usually the one that was in use before the intended font change. There are two possible explanations of this error. One is that the font name was mis-spelt in the header. The following line in the header, for instance, will cause this error:

\F2 Trinity.Bodl 12

Clearly "Trinity.Bold" was intended, but the computer will faithfully search for a directory called "Trinity.BodI" which it will not find.

Make certain that you spell font names correctly. If you are unsure about the spelling of a font name you can get a list of the current contents of /Fonts while in !Edit by selecting "Display" from the main menu.

The same error is generated, of course, if you deliberately specify a font name that does not exist. For instance, if you delete a font from !Fonts and later attempt to reload a !Draw file that uses it in a text area object.

Line numbers in text files

The line numbers given in error messages relating to text files can be useful in locating the cause of the error. In !Edit a "line" is a string of any number of characters terminated by <CR>; it may occupy many lines on the screen. In fact it is often useful to think of it as a paragraph. The first line in the text file (the one which generally reads "\! 1") is line 0.

Problems in !Draw

Wrong font used in text object

If an item in a text object appears in the system font rather than the originally chosen font, check that the original font is still in !Fonts. If a font is deleted from !Fonts or its name changed, !Draw will default to the system font in the affected text object.

Text wrong shape in text object

If, in a text object, the text appears to be very condensed, that is, very tall and narrow, almost certainly you set the text height in mistake for the text size. By default the text size is 6.4 pt with the outline font manager. If you wanted 14 pt text but, by an easily made mistake, selected this from the Text height sub-menu rather than the text size sub-menu, you will get characters which have 14 pt height combined with 6.4 pt width. The solution is to enter the Text size sub-menu and set the size to 14 pt before you complete the object.

Rules print out crooked, although straight on display

Since the printer is capable of a higher resolution display than the screen, it sometimes shows up faults which the screen is not capable of displaying. When you use the path object procedures to create vertical and horizontal rules, always use the "Grid Lock" facility. This will ensure that all rules are exactly vertical or horizontal. If you create your rules "free-hand" judging them from the screen display, they may end up slightly out of true–so slightly that the screen cannot display it. The printer, however, may have the resolution to show it as an unsightly series of "steps" in the rule. This can be corrected by selecting "Grid Lock" and Select mode and using the "Snap to Grid" facility.

Transferred object is missing

To transfer an object from one !Draw window to another (unless they relate to the same sheet) it is necessary to select the object concerned and save it into the other window. Unfortunately objects transferred in this way are often hard to locate in their new window. This is because '.Draw places the imported object at the current pointer position offset by the object's original position; this may well be outside the paper limits.

The way to find such a missing object is as follows. In the window which received the object enter Select mode and from the Select sub- menu choose "Select all". Next, from the "Paper limits" sub-menu (attained from "Misc") choose AO. From the main menu slide off

"Zoom" and reduce the magnification until the screen displays the errant object neatly highlighted by its boundary box. Clear the selection and then select just the offending object. Then, drag it into the main drawing area and restore the page size and magnification to normal.

Scrolling and/or printing is slow

Scrolling gets slower as you put more objects or text on the page, but if you find it excessive (eg over a minute from top to bottom of a page of A4) check the size of the font cache using the Task Display. This should be at least 64K and if you are using many fonts make it larger than that, as large as possible. Too small a font cache will have a devastating effect on scrolling (and printing) speed as the computer will need to repeatedly access the disc for font data in order to write the text.

If you have a hard disc, put your ! Fonts application on it, in the root directory. Access is faster from a hard disc than from floppies. Moreover on a hard disc you can put many more fonts in the /Fonts directory.

Avoid using the "zoom" facility to get an enlarged view of text. It is fine with graphics but with text it can easily quadruple scrolling times! But by all means open a "New view" window with a reduced-scale zoom so you can see the whole document; this will not need to scroll and adds little to the time burden.

It also helps if you lay out your "body text", ie the main bulk of the document in a smallish typeface, first. This will probably only use one, two or perhaps three fonts. When satisfied with its layout, put in larger titles, headings, captions and by-lines using text objects.

Printing is a slow process at the best of times. (Incidentally !Draw is no slower than the "proper" DTP packages, all of which print using very similar procedures.) The computer divides the sheet into "strips" of bitmap which are sent to the printer for printing as graphics.

Clearly, the higher the resolution of the printer, the greater the amount of data that must be sent and the higher the number of calculations that the computer must perform to derive them. A page of well utilised A4 at 300 dpi involves the calculation and transmission to the printer of nearly 1 Megabyte of data.

If there is not enough memory available for even one such "strip" to be compiled, obviously printing cannot begin and the computer gives a suitable error message.

If there is enough memory for one strip, every object on the sheet will be examined to see if it affects the strip about to be printed. If it does, the object is plotted on to the strip as though it were a virtual screen having the same resolution as the printer. When all objects have been examined, the strip is printed and the entire process is repeated for the next strip. The cycle continues until the sheet has been printed.

Printing also takes longer if your page layout is "landscape" (horizontal) rather than "portrait" (vertical). This is because the font manager assumes portrait orientation and the data concerning character outlines must be converted to landscape format.

Cannot "select" an object (1)

The "select" facility in !Draw does not work as well as the User Manual suggests, especially when you have a large number of overlapping objects including portions of text area. A useful trick when you simply cannot select that deeply nested portion of text area is to take the pointer to a nearby position on the edge of the page (so that it is not actually over any object), hold the "select" button down and "pull out" a selected area which embraces the object you wish to select. All objects overlapping the pulled-out area become selected. You can then cancel those you do not wish to select.

Alternatively, use the "Select" sub-menu's "Select All" option and then cancel all the unwanted objects by clicking ADJUST on them. It's time consuming but it never fails!

Cannot "select" an object (2)

Sometimes it can be apparently impossible to select a certain object even in a relatively uncluttered !Draw window and even using the method described above. Probably, when you attempt to select the object in question, a different object overlapping it is becoming selected, although you may not notice this at first. When this happens, check to see if the two objects concerned have become "grouped". Leaving the "wrong" object selected, call up the "Select" sub-menu and see if "Ungroup" is one of the options available. If so, select it and then de-select the "wrong" object. You should now find that the object you originally wished to select is selected. It is quite easy for selected objects to become grouped unintentionally. Most often this is caused by the pointer moving by accident over the "Group" option of the "Select" sub-menu just before you click the mouse intending to perform some other operation.

Cannot edit path object

You cannot edit a path object that has been grouped. Clicking ADJUST on the object will have no effect until it has been ungrouped.

Words missing

You may sometimes find that the first word or first few words are omitted from a text area, both on screen and in printout. This happens if you have specified a larger font than will fit the line spacing–such as a 24 pt font in a heading while the line spacing is only 12 pt. !Draw will decide it has no room and will omit all or part of the offending text. It is easiest to leave headings out of text areas and insert them "by hand" into !Draw as text objects when the body text is in place.

Problems with Printing

Printer delivers gobbledegook

If your printer delivers strings of carriage returns interspersed with seemingly random characters, check first that you have loaded the correct printer driver and, if so, that you have chosen a graphics mode appropriate to your printer. The graphics mode is chosen by clicking SELECT on the printer driver icon and then clicking SELECT or ADJUST in the graphics mode window until the appropriate mode is displayed. Bv clicking MENU on the printer driver and then selecting "Save options" you can save your choice. The printer driver will thereafter start up with your chosen graphics mode selected.

Lines of text missing from printout

Sometimes large chunks of body text may be missing from a printout. On several occasions all the body text was missing from one of my documents! Graphics and headings were faithfully printed in the right places–only the text was missing, though it appeared quite normally on the screen. On another occasion, the last four lines of body text in each column were missing. This appears to be a "bug" possibly caused by interference from other software. The "fix" is to save any unsaved material, switch off the machine, leave it for 10 seconds, then switch on and start again from scratch. Chances are your printout will now be normal. It is always advisable to switch off your computer to clear its memory before a !Draw/ !Edit session.

Descenders not printed

The descenders (below-the-line parts of such characters as "p" and "g") are sometimes missing from some lines of text when you use outline fonts in conjunction with the earlier printer drivers. The earlier printer drivers were not fully compatible with outline fonts. The fix is to obtain a more recent printer driver such as version 1.12 on the RISC OS 2.00 extras disc.

Dot matrix printout is distorted

On a dot matrix printer at high graphics resolution (such as an FX-80 at 240 x 216 dpi) the right-hand edges of the characters may appear slightly "ragged". Examine, for instance, the letter y printed with the paper in "portrait" orientation. This is an inevitable consequence of the way in which the printer works and is explained in Chapter 10. In "landscape" printing the distortion is forced into the top edge of the characters, where, though still visible, it is much less noticeable. Examine, for instance, a "T" printed this way.

13 : The Next Step

There is no doubt that !Draw and !Edit in conjunction with the outline font system can form the basis of a most effective low-cost DTP system. I have used it extensively to produce publications ranging from magazines and brochures to software user manuals. And I know of other Archimedes users who have made similar use of it.

Full-feature DTP software

DTP using !Draw and !Edit is, however, rather like a self-catering holiday. Everything works and is enjoyable enough, but sooner or later you hanker for the convenience of someone else to relieve you of the mundane chores! Probably you will end up by upgrading to one of the commercial full-feature DTP systems.

What improvements can you expect from such an upgrade? And how much of the ancillary software that you have amassed will still be of use to you then?

The answer to the second question is simple enough–all of it. All of your outline fonts, any clip art, any logos or other designs that you have created in !Draw or !Paint, your printer drivers and such utilities as !FontFX and !FontEd will be as useful to you then as now. !Draw itself will still be useful since it offers drawing facilities far more sophisticated than those in any of the DTP packages. All the DTP packages allow !Draw files to be imported and used as part of (or even the whole of) a DTP document.

Not only the software but also the experience you have gained on !Draw will be useful. All four packages, for example, will run on a 1 Megabyte machine, but memory may be very tight. Consequently such tricks as deleting the printer driver (you may need to delete it before you can even load the DTP application) and changing to Mode 0 to accelerate printing will still apply.

The answer to the first question is–many! There are two principal differences between DTP using a full DTP package and the "improvised" variety using /Draw and !Edit. Firstly, text handling is far simpler. There is no longer any distinction between text objects and text area objects. You can simply create a text frame wherever you wish to put text and type your text into it. The frame may contain a one line heading or a whole chapter of a book. Instead of typing in the text you can import into the text frame text files already created in !Edit or other applications. Full editing facilities are provided including a "search and replace" function. Indeed you can use a DTP package as though it were a sophisticated wordprocessor if you wish. There is, of course, a full choice of outline fonts and you can change fonts as often as you wish. All the packages allow you to highlight a passage and change it to a different font such as italic or bold or a different size. You could achieve the same using !Draw and !Edit, but it would be a far more complex sequence of operations involving the transfer of files between the two applications.

Secondly, frames normally "repel" other frames. If, for instance, you move a picture frame so that it overlaps a text frame, instead of simply covering it, or being hidden behind it, as would happen in !Draw, the text automatically reformats itself neatly around the picture frame. To achieve the same effect in /Draw and !Edit would involve the creation of several "columns" of varying sizes and their careful positioning around the picture.

Another feature is that the DTP packages allow you to save stylesheets set up for frequently used page layouts. If you edit a club, church or school magazine this is a most useful facility. They also allow you to define and save paragraph styles which specify the font, style, size, leading and degree of first-line indentation. Often you can change paragraph style at a press of a function key. All the DTP packages are true RISC OS applications fully conforming to the RISC OS philosophy with which you should by now be fully acquainted. All are object-based like !Draw. The "objects" are generally the frames which may be text frames or picture frames. Rules are also objects. The way in which pages are redrawn object by object will remind you over and over again of !Draw. All the DTP packages contain the facility to import sprites and !Draw files, but most will not accept !Draw files containing text areas.

Let's examine the four packages in sequence. The following are emphatically not complete reviews (unfortunately I was unable to obtain review copies of two of them) and so I cannot attempt to mention all the features of the packages. To do so would quadruple the length of this book! The reviews concentrate on the differences between the packages rather than the features they have in common.

Appendix

A Glossary of DTP, Printing and Typographical Terms

- Accent - A small symbol superimposed on a letter, normally denoting the way in which it should be pronounced. In English, accents are only used in words of foreign origin such as cafe, naive and Noel. In most European languages accented characters are quite common. Acorn outline fonts include a wide range of accented characters allowing most European languages to be reproduced correctly.

- Anti-aliasing - Use of intermediate shades on the screen to overcome the screen's lack of resolution. When fonts are reproduced on the screen, anti-aliasing helps to smooth out the "steps" that would otherwise appear in diagonal strokes (such as the main strokes in the letter "A").

- ASCII - American Standard Code for Information Interchange. A code in which letters, numerals, punctuation marks and other symbols are represented by numbers. All computers use ASCII although considerable variations do exist. The original ASCII code was a 7-bit code involving numbers from 0 to 127. Codes 0 to 31 are "control" codes which control cursor movement and other effects. Codes 32 to 126 are printable characters. Code 127 represents "Delete". In the Acorn outline fonts, codes 128 to 255 are also allocated to printable characters which greatly extends the range of characters available.

- Bezier curves - The system used in !Draw's path objects for storing data concerning curved lines. Each line is defined by the coordinates of its start and finish and the coordinates of two "control points", one relating to each end of the line.

- Bit - The direction of the control point from the line end indicates the direction of the curve at that end of the line. The distance of the control point from the end of the line is inversely proportional to the rate at which the curve diverges from its original direction. Short for "binary digit". The smallest possible unit of data, each bit being either equal to 0 or to 1.

- Bit-image or Bitmap - Representation of graphics or typefaces by dividing their shapes into equal sized dots which are stored as digital data, often with one bit representing each dot.

- Body text - The main portion of text in an article, brochure or book as opposed to headings and figure captions.

- Bold - Text in an emphasised form, appearing darker than ordinary text. Bold is used for emphasis, for example, in headings.

- Byte - The smallest unit of data that a computer can independently access. It consists of eight bits and may be regarded as representing a number between 0 and 255.

- Caption - A short piece of text identifying the contents of an adjacent picture, diagram or table.

- Caret - A special form of cursor used in software handling proportionally spaced characters. In !Edit and !Draw it is a red vertical bar whose serif-like extensions at each end make it resemble a capital "I". The next character to be printed appears just to the right of the caret. Centering   Positioning the text so that it falls exactly midway between the margins, giving a symmetrical effect.

- Clip art - A collection of drawings and half tones supplied in the form of sprites or path objects for ad lib reproduction in the user's publications.

- Collating - Collecting together the pages of a publication in the right order before stapling or binding.

- Condensed text - Characters that are narrower than normal. Cropping Trimming the edges of a picture so that the required subject appears in the centre.

- Cursor - In a word processor a mobile indicator of the point at which the next character will appear on the screen. It may or may not blink; it may take the form of an underline or square of different colour.

- Descender - Part of a character which extends below the "line" on which the character is considered as sitting. Examples are the tails of such characters as "g", "p" and "y".

- Dither pattern - A pattern of pixels of alternating colours used to achieve the effect of intermediate colours. Examples can be seen by using the RISC OS Desktop environment in screen Mode 0; dither patterns of black and white are used to represent various shades of grey.

- Dot matrix printer - A kind of printer which prints text or graphics on paper by building up a pattern of dots. The dots are created by blows from the wires (usually 9 or 24 in number) in the print head via an inked ribbon.

- Drop capital - An oversize capital letter at the start of a paragraph. It usually occupies the start of the first three or four lines.

- Drop shadow - A black or grey simulated shadow behind text or graphics in a box giving the illusion that the box is floating in space above the page.

- Em - A unit of length at one time used by printers, equal to 1/6 inch or 12 points. It is so named because at one time it was regarded as the standard width of a 12 point capital "M". The unit is not often used today, but its name persists in the "em dash", a dash of supposedly the same length as a capital "M".

- Em dash (–) - ASCII code 152 in Acorn outline fonts. A punctuation mark used in place of commas for expressing apposition. Example: "The BBC Microcomputer – a machine at one time very popular in education – had only 32 Kbytes of RAM".

- En dash (-) - ASCII code 151 in Acorn outline fonts. A punctuation mark used in place of the word "to" in such expressions as "the 1939-1945 war".

- Figure (1) - A numeral as opposed to an alphabetical character, a punctuation mark or symbol.

- Figure (2) - A diagram, drawing or photograph illustrating an article or publication.

- Font - A complete set of typographical characters of uniform style and size. They are generally known by names such as "Trinity Medium". • Footline - A line at the foot of the page in magazines giving the magazine title (normally on the left-hand pages) and issue date (normally on the right-hand pages).

- Graphics - Any material which can appear on a printed page or on a monitor screen which does not consist of text. Graphics includes lines, boxes, circles, geometrical shapes, line drawings, sprites and half tones.

- Half tone - An illustration which uses many intermediate shades between the current ink colour and the current paper colour. Photographs reproduced for printing are "screened" into dots whose size determines the apparent shade of the area—larger dots will appear darker. The laser printer drivers for the Archimedes include routines which convert sprites for half tone reproduction. This allows images captured by scanners to be incorporated into DTP and !Draw documents.

- Hanging indent - A form of paragraph setting in which the first line of the paragraph is full width and subsequent lines are indented.

- Heading - A title or subtitle usually distinguished from body text by use of a different style or size of print.

- Headline - A very large heading designed to attract the reader's attention to an important item.

- Icon - A small picture provided as a sprite which is used on screen to represent an application, utility or facility provided by an application. To start the application or use the facility, the mouse is moved so that the pointer is over the application and then the SELECT button on the mouse is clicked.

- Indent - Moving the left-hand edge of the text to the right. An indent may apply to just one line, as often used at the start of paragraphs, or over many lines, eg in quoted matter or in hanging indents.

- Inferior - See subscript

- Ink jet printer - A kind of printer which forms characters from dots made by blowing tiny jets of ink on to the paper. Quality is very variable, but some types give results almost as good as a laser printer.

- Italics - Slanted text thus: italics. Italics are used to emphasise passages, sometimes to represent quoted matter and often to represent titles or foreign words. Justified   Text which is "justified"–some call it "doubly justified"–has its right-hand and left-hand margins perfectly straight. The widths of the word spaces are adjusted to make all lines the same length, except in lines which fall at the end of paragraphs.

- Kilobyte (Kbyte) - A unit of data equal to 1024 bytes. Landscape Use of paper with the longer sides horizontal, as on most "landscape" paintings. !Draw supports landscape pages, but scrolling and printing take much longer than for the alternative, portrait pages.

- Laser printer - A type of printer which produces very high quality text and graphics very quickly. Its main disadvantage is its cost.

- Leading - The space between lines of text on a printed page, so called because at one time strips of lead alloy in standard thicknesses of 1 point or 2 point were inserted to space out lines regarded as too close.

- Ligature - A compound character consisting of two characters joined together Examples are the "fi" and "fl" characters found in ASCII codes 158 and 159 Acorn outline fonts.

- Lithography - A form ot printing which relies on the immiscibility of water and oil. An image of the page is formed on the flat surface of a "plate" as a pattern of areas of water and oil- based ink. See also offset lithography.

- Margin - The area of normally unprinted space between the page contents and the edges of the page.

- Megabyte (MByte) - A unit of data equal to 1024 Kbytes or 1,048,576 bytes.

- Mouse - A piece of hardware which is used to move a pointer, caret or the cross-hairs on the screen to provide fine control of graphics functions as well as for selecting facilities indicated by icons.

- Non-Break Space (NBSP) - A character (code 160) which appears identical to a normal space (code 32) but which is treated by applications as a normal printed character in that lines cannot be split at a NBSP. It is also useful in providing paragraph indents in justified text since the width of the NBSP is fixed, whereas that of the normal space varies in justified text.

- Object - In !Draw any item in a drawing is an object or part of an object. A !Draw file consists of a sequence of "segments" each describing an object and containing sufficient data to allow that object to be reproduced. One object may overlap another and may totally obscure it. Oblique   The name used for italics in some fonts.

- Offset lithography - The most commonly used method of printing books, magazines and newspapers. The image on the plate is formed as in conventional lithography, but the plate is wrapped around a cylinder and a rubber blanket roller transfers the image to the paper. The resulting rotary machine is capable of faster operation than conventional reciprocating presses.

- Outline font system - A system of font management in which details of the characters in each font are stored as plotting instructions. This has the advantage that any size of character can be produced without loss of resolution.

- Path object - In !Draw an object composed of one or more "paths" which may be straight lines, curved lines or moves which do not draw lines.

- Photocopier - A machine that produces copies of documents by an essentially photographic/electrostatic process. A photocopier may be used to produce multiple copies of documents produced by DTP quite economically.

- Pi-font - Jargon for a font containing special symbols rather than the normal alpha-numerics and punctuation marks. Examples are Acorn's Selwyn based on Zapf Dingbats and Beebug's SymbolB.

- Pixel - The smallest possible portion of a computer screen. On the Archimedes, a Mode 12 screen consists of 256 rows each containing 640 pixels. Each pixel is approximately twice as tall as it is broad and may be in any of 16 colours which, by default, include black, white, six intermediate shades of grey and eight colours. As each pixel in this mode offers 16 colour possibilities four bits are needed to store it. The characteristics of pixels will vary from screen mode to screen mode. In Mode 20, for instance, the colours are the same as Mode 12, but there are 512 rows of pixels, each being approximately square; Mode 20 offers twice the vertical resolution of Mode 12 but also uses twice as much memory. • Plate - In litho printing a sheet of paper, plastic or metal on to which the image of the page being printed is transferred by photocopying.

- Point - A unit of length still widely used in the printing and associated industries. One point equals 1/72 inch. Font sizes are specified in points, the number of points representing the distance from the apex of the tallest character in the font to the bottom of the longest descender. For body text in books, magazines and newspapers, fonts of size 7 to 10 points are most frequently used.

- Pointer - An arrow on the screen which is moved as the mouse is moved on the desktop.

- Portrait - Use of paper with its longer sides vertical as in most "portrait" paintings.

- Printer - A piece of hardware which puts text or graphics on paper in response to the computer. See laser, dot matrix and ink jet.

- Printer driver - A piece of software which processes the data being sent to the printer, ensuring that it is in a suitable format.

- Proportional spacing - The characters used on standard typewriters and also the "system font" in the Archimedes/A3000 computers all have the same width. In most typefaces used in professional printing, however, the characters have various widths according to their design. Compare, for instance, the width of an "i" and that of a "W". Proportionally spaced systems allow characters to have as much or as little width as their design demands.

- Ranged left - Sometimes called "unjustified". Text printed with a straight left margin and ragged right margin, as on a standard typewriter.

- Ranged right - Sometimes called "fully indented". Text printed with a straight right margin and ragged left margin.

- Roman text - Normal upright text as opposed to italic or oblique.

- Sans-serif - A typeface in which the characters lack serifs. Best known examples are the Helvetica-style fonts such as Acorn's "Homerton" family or Beebug's "SwissB".

- Scanner - A device which converts paper documents to machine- readable data. Inexpensive hand scanners are simply moved over the document, an image appearing on the screen of the text or graphics on the document. More sophisticated scanners incorporate document feed facilities, giving more accurate conversion of data. The associated software for the Archimedes allows the captured image to be saved as sprites which can be edited in IPaint and incorporated into !Draw documents.

- Screendump - The process of copying the contents of the current monitor display (or the pixel structure of a sprite) to a printer, whereby each pixel or group of pixels is represented by a dot or group of dots on the paper.

- Screening - The process used by the printing trade to convert areas of solid grey or colour to a pattern of black and white dots that can be printed satisfactorily. !Draw does provide a form of crude screening when printing out coloured or intermediate grey matter.

- Scrolling - Movement of the entire screen contents so that in a wordprocessor, DTP or art program, for example, another part of the document is seen.

- Serif - A protrusion at the end of a stroke in a character to give it style and make it easier to read. Note the serifs, four in all, at each of a capital "1" in a serif font such as Acorn's Trinity" family. There are also typeface styles which lack serifs and are commonly referred to as "sans-serif" fonts.

- Sprite - A graphical object in which the information describing it is held as a series of numbers defining the colours of all the pixels within it. A portion of a screen or even a whole screen can be saved as a sprite. The Archimedes has a very sophisticated sprite handling system which allows sprites created in one screen mode to be displayed in other screen modes. Sprites can be created and edited in the RISC-OS application i.Paint.

- Subscript (or inferior) - Characters written below the line level and normally in a smaller typeface, as in chemical formulae.

- Superscript (or superior) - Characters written above the line level and normally in a smaller typeface, as in indices and exponentials, eg 1,000,000 = $1 \times 10^{6} = 1 \times 106$.

- Table, tabular matter - Matter displayed in rows and columns such as mathematical tables, transport timetables, tables of contacts' names and telephone numbers or the results of scientific experiments.

- Text - A portion of data consisting of printable characters (numbers, letters, punctuation marks and other symbols) which in a computer would be stored as a string of ASCII codes.

- Text area object - In !Draw an area of the document displaying text created in !Edit and using a special format. The size of the characters is determined by commands in the text; resizing the text area in !Draw simply causes the text to rearrange itself within the area without changing the size of the characters themselves.

- Text object - In !Draw an object containing a line of text entered at the keyboard using '.Draw's own text facility. Resizing a text object alters the size and possibly the proportions of the characters in the text object.
- Toner - The powdered ink used in photocopiers and laser printers. It is transferred to the paper via a roller electrostatically and is fused into the paper by heat.
- Unjustified - See "Ranged left".

This book was produced using an Acorn Risc PC; from files originally produced by David Holden. Visit www.apdl.org.uk to download many of the software titles mentioned.

www.ingramcontent.com/pod-product-compliance
Lightning Source LLC
Chambersburg PA
CBHW070400290526
45790CB00004B/1568